Biblical Lovemaking

a study
of the
Song of Solomon

P.O. BOX 3723 • TUSTIN, CA 92680

Arnold G. Fruchtenbaum

אריאל ARIEL
PRESS
P.O. BOX 3226
SAN ANTONIO, TEXAS 78213

Other Books by Arnold G. Fruchtenbaum

Jesus Was A Jew
Hebrew Christianity: Its Theology, History, and Philosophy
The Footsteps of the Messiah: A Study of the Sequence of Prophetic Events
A Hebrew Christian Passover Haggadah

This volume is dedicated to my own Shulamit

MARY ANN

in all the spirit of *Ahavah*

TABLE OF CONTENTS

INTRODUCTION

1:1

INTRODUCTION

1:1

The English text has titled this book as *The Song of Solomon.* The Hebrew text, however, reads:

The Song of Songs,
Which is Solomon's

In the Hebrew construction there is a repetition of the noun in the genetive, thus making it a superlative. It is *THE* Song of Songs, the one song surpassing all other songs. The song is one of many composed by Solomon and of his 1,005 songs (I Kings 4:32), it is the choicest of his songs. This is the force of the Hebrew construction.

Similar Hebrew superlatives are found in expressions such as *Holy of Holies* (that is, the Most Holy), *vanity of vanities* (that is, the most vain), the King of Kings (that is, the greatest of all kings). The point of the construction is to emphasize choiceness.

This very construction explains the high Jewish attitude towards this book of the Bible. Rabbi Akiba, a leading rabbi of the Bar Cochba Revolt (132-135 A.D.) stated, "No day in the whole history of the world is worth so much as that in which the Song of Songs was given: for all the writings are holy, but the Song of Songs is the Holy of Holies" (Mesilla 7a). In another place Rabbi Akiba said, "The whole world attained its supreme value only on the day when the Song of Songs was given to Israel" (Mishnah Yadaim 3:5).

Yet in spite of this high view of the book, because of its erotic content, the rabbis forbade the book to be read by anyone under the age of thirty. But once proper age had been attained, the *Midrash Rabbah* points out the importance of giving attention to the message of this book:

Had any other man composed them, it would have been incumbent on you to incline your ear and to listen to them; all the more since Solomon composed them. Had he composed them out of his own mind, it would have been incumbent on you to incline your ear and listen to them; all the more then since he composed them in the Holy Spirit.

Theories of Interpretation

The most common theory among evangelicals and Jewish commentators is the *Allegorical* theory of interpretation. The book is not taken as a true historical account of two lovers, but rather that the two lovers are symbolic of something else. What that "something else" is, is not totally agreed upon by the allegorical school. But there are two basic views in the allegorical approach. One view sees the allegory as representing God's love for Israel. This has been the view of the majority of Jewish commentators as well as a great number of evangelicals. The other variation, held by many other evangelicals, sees the allegory as representing Christ's love for the Church.

Very similar to the allegorical approach is the *Typical* interpretation. This view accepts a real historical base to the story but then makes the base a type of God's love for Israel or Christ's love for the Church. Most commentaries from this school deal with the antitype, while the historical account itself is largely ignored. This view is followed by a great many evangelicals such as Ironside and others.

The present author does not feel that either of the above theories of interpretation is correct but prefers the *Literal* interpretation view, since it is the most self-consistent view and does not allow for runaway imagination. This view interprets the book normally, as the love relationship between a man and a woman. The book describes the courtship, marriage, wedding night, and subsequent sexual adjustments of the young couple. These are real historical situations through which God intends to teach lessons regarding the divine viewpoint in the very areas of courtship, marriage, and sex, just as other historical books of the Bible teach us divine principles in other areas.

In accordance with the literal view, the Song of Solomon must be viewed as a collection of erotic songs or idylls of love which were put together on the basis of a literary merit and not on the basis of allegorical or typical meanings. The purpose is to describe ideal human love and to give God's viewpoint of sexual love within marriage, and this it does in some explicit ways. It is for this very reason that many have shied away from the literal approach and have taken an allegorical or typical approach. The allegorical approach allows for a complete bypassing of the erotic passages, while the typical approach only needs to admit that they are there and then can immediately pursue the type itself. But this means entering into exposition with preconceived notions and prejudices. Since the Scriptures have much to say about God's rules of conduct in every other area of human relations, is it so difficult to believe and expect that God could have something to say of sexual behavior? Especially since this is the most intimate relationship a man and a woman can enter into? The author feels that this is exactly what God through this book has done.

The basic lessons to be derived from this book are as follows:

1. No form of sexual behavior is unclean, invalid, or sinful between a married couple.

2. The guiding rule, however, is that all such behavior meet two standards:
   a. It is agreeable to both partners and not just to one.
   b. It meets the mate's needs.

3. However, any form of sexual behavior found in the Song of Solomon only means it is valid for a married couple. It does not mean the practice is mandatory, but voluntary on the basis of the two standards mentioned above.

The Form of the Song

The form that the Song of Solomon is written in can be classed as a *lyric idyll.* In this format there is a collection of songs, events, or speeches, but the sequence as found in the collection is not necessarily chronological. However, there is a story in the background. The poet then selects certain events, dialogues, or speeches from the historical background and puts them together on the basis of a literary merit or style without regard to the sequence in which they actually occurred. Furthermore, there is also the presence of a chorus which is an imaginary group that interrupts certain scenes to make brief speeches, or to give a warning, or are just brought in to allow for the carrying on of a discussion.

The Song of Solomon clearly follows the format of a lyric idyll. The story in the background concerns the courtship, marriage, wedding night and subsequent sexual adjustments of Solomon and his bride, Shulamit. Solomon, the author and poet of the Song of Songs, selected five events from the historical background and put them together into five idylls on the basis of literary merit and not on the basis of the sequence of events. These five idylls* are as follows:

> 1:2 – 2:7
> 2:8 – 3:5
> 3:6 – 5:1
> 5:2 – 6:9
> 6:10 – 8:14

Furthermore, Solomon records the story not from his own perspective but from the perspective of the bride. In the book *she* is the one who is telling the story. It is the bride who is relating the five idylls. Also, she tells this story by means of reflections as she recounts her days of courtship, marriage and early married life. There are thirteen such reflections** in the book, and they are as follows:

> 1:2-8
> 1:9-14
> 1:15–2:7
> 2:8-17
> 3:1-5
> 3:6-11
> 4:1–5:1
> 5:2–6:3
> 6:4-9
> 6:10–7:10

---

* Keil and Delitzsch, however, see six idylls as follows: 1:1-2:7, 2:8-3:5, 3:6-5:1, 5:2-6:9, 6:10-8:4, 8:5-14. The author feels that the last two should be taken together.

** Keil and Delitzsch divide their six idylls into two scenes each making a total of twelve scenes: 1:1-8, 1:9-2:7, 2:8-17, 3:1-5, 3:6-11, 4:1-5:1, 5:2-6:3, 6:4-9, 6:10-7:6, 7:7-8:4, 8:5-7, 8:8-14.

7:11–8:4
8:5-7
8:8-14

The relationship of the thirteen reflections to the five idylls will be brought out in the outline to follow.

Finally, in keeping with the lyric idyll motif, there is the presence of the imaginary chorus known as the *Daughters of Jerusalem.*

The Story Behind The Song

The key factor is the historical background to the song. What is the story behind the song? Those who accept the literal approach to the book often disagree as to whether there are two or three major characters in the book.

Those who accept the *three major character view* see the three as being Solomon, Shulamit, and an unnamed shepherd. In their account of the story, Shulamit and the unnamed shepherd are in love and in courtship. Solomon, seeing Shulamit, falls in love with her and forces her against her will to come with him to Jerusalem to make her one of his many wives. Once they arrive in the palace of Jerusalem, Solomon speaks words of love to Shulamit hoping to win her love with his words and his gifts to her. But Shulamit remains true to her shepherd and echoes Solomon's words of love with her own words of love for the shepherd. Solomon, finally seeing that he will never win the love of Shulamit, allows her to return to her home and to her shepherd lover.

This view is held in common by liberal theologians, who already start out with a low view of the Bible. The three character view causes confusion in many of the sections and reduces the erotic scenes to mere immoral actions inconsistent with the high moral conduct required by the holiness of God. The erotic passages become nothing but pre-marital lust rather than the beauty of sexual relations within marriage. The three character view is unacceptable for these very reasons.

The *two major character view* is far more consistent with the high view of inspiration. The two characters are Solomon and Shulamit.

In the story behind the song, Solomon owns a vineyard in Lower Galilee near the town of Shunem. One day, while visiting his vineyards, he meets a farm girl as she is taking care of her own family vineyard. The family consists of a mother, a younger sister, and at least two older brothers. The father is presumed to be dead for he is never mentioned. She is found working in the vineyards, because her brothers became angry with her and forced her to work in the family vineyard under the scorching hot sun, that in the course of time gave her a dark and swarthy complexion.

Solomon falls in love with her and begins courting her and visiting her in her country home. She finally agrees to marry him. Shortly before the wedding, Solomon sends a wedding procession to bring the bride to his palace in Jerusalem. After her arrival, the wedding ceremony takes place, followed by the wedding banquet and then the wedding night, which is erotically described.

Later the problems of sexual adjustment arise. One night Shulamit rejects Solomon's sexual advances, and so the king leaves. Shulamit repents and begins to search for him. After finding him, they have a loving reunion.

After some time in the palace, Shulamit begins to yearn for a visit to her home, a request to which Solomon agrees. They make a visit to her home where they renew their love covenant, and the book closes with the enjoyment of sexual love in their mountain home.

This is the historical background in chronological sequence. But since the song is in the form of a lyric idyll, while all these elements of the story will be found in the song, they are not related in this particular chronological sequence. The historical sequence, as noted above, can only be deduced after a study of the five idylls and the thirteen reflections involved.

Shulamit in Hebrew is merely the feminine form of the masculine name of *Solomon.* Shulamit is to Solomon what Pauline is to Paul. Thus the story behind the song is the story of Solomon and Shulamit or "Mr. and Mrs. Solomon."

The entire book will only make sense with a two character view.

The Outline

I. Courtship and Marriage   1:2–5:1

    A. FIRST IDYLL: The Wedding Day Reflections   1:2–2:7
        1. First Reflection: Shulamit Preparing for the Wedding Feast   1:2-8
        2. Second Reflection: At the Wedding Feast   1:9-14
        3. Third Reflection: In the Bridal Chamber   1:15–2:7

    B. SECOND IDYLL: The Courtship Period Reflections   2:8–3:5
        1. Fourth Reflection: A Springtime Visit   2:8-17
        2. Fifth Reflection: Dreams of Separation   3:1-5

    C. THIRD IDYLL: Marital Union Reflections   3:6–5:1
        1. Sixth Reflection: The Wedding Procession 3:6-11
        2. Seventh Reflection: The Wedding Night   4:1–5:1

II. Sexual Adjustments in Marriage   5:2–8:14

    A. FOURTH IDYLL: Sexual Problem Reflections 5:2–6:9
        1. Eighth Reflection: Shulamit's Troubled Dream of Love Refused   5:2–6:3
        2. Ninth Reflection: The Return of Solomon   6:4-9

This treatment of the Song of Solomon will follow the above out-line. The translation of the Song of Solomon is the author's own directly from the Hebrew. All other biblical quotations are taken from the American Standard Version of 1901. In dealing with each reflection, the first part will be the exegesis and *exposition* of the book. The exposition of such reflection will be followed by a *summary* of the content of the reflection. Then will come the *application* of the text where all the principles of the Song of Solomon will be applied to the Christian family life structure. Since this study is limited to the Song of Solomon, other principles found elsewhere in Scripture will not be discussed. However, these can be found in two very good books by Tim Timmons: *God's Plan For Your Marriage* (Baker Book House) and *Maximum Marriage* (Revell).*

Three people deserve my special thanks in the writing of this book. First is Tim Timmons, who stimulated me and encouraged me to make a study of The Song of Solomon from the Hebrew and develop this approach. Secondly, to my wife, Mary Ann, who corrected the manu-script and made many useful suggestions along with some good insights. Thirdly, to Mrs. Jean Cooper for being so kind as to type the manuscript.

* See Appendix for a list of recommended books on the subject.

PART ONE

COURTSHIP AND MARRIAGE

1:2 - 5:1

CHAPTER ONE

THE FIRST IDYLL: THE WEDDING DAY REFLECTIONS
1:2 - 2:7

The first idyll contains three reflections all taking place on Solomon's and Shulamit's wedding day. The first reflection takes place shortly after the wedding ceremony as Shulamit is getting ready for the wedding feast. The second reflection takes place at the wedding feast itself, while the third is after the wedding feast in the bridal chamber.

Reflection One: Shulamit Preparing for the Wedding Feast
1:2-8

This reflection opens the book with Shulamit in the palace getting ready for the wedding feast and the wedding night to follow. The wedding ceremony has already taken place.

The first reflection begins with Shulamit speaking to the imaginary chorus of the Daughters of Jerusalem as she expresses her longing to be with her new husband as she looks forward to her wedding night. Shulamit's opening speech is found in 1:2-4a.

(2) Let him kiss me with the kisses of his mouth,
        For your love is better than wine.
(3) To the smell, your ointments are good,
        Like poured out oil is your name,
     On account of this the virgins love you.
(4a) Draw me — After you let us run.
        The king has brought me into his chamber.

The Song of Songs begins as Shulamit expresses two desires. The first desire is "Let him kiss me" (vs. 2a). She gives two reasons for this first desire. First, Solomon's love is better than wine (vs. 2b), and secondly, because of the fragrance of that love (vs. 3).

Throughout the Song of Songs, three different Hebrew words for love will be used, all of which are translated by the English word "love," but they do not all mean the same kind of love. The first Hebrew word is *dod,* which is equivalent to the Greek *eros* and refers to sexual love. The second Hebrew word is *ahavah,* which is equivalent to the Greek *agapei* and refers to the love of the will. Thus *dod* is to *ahavah* in Hebrew what *eros* is to *agapei* in Greek. Both *ahavah* and *agapei* cover a wide spectrum and might include the element of sexual love, but are not limited to it as *dod* and *eros* would be. The third Hebrew word is *ra'eyah,* equivalent to the Greek *phileo,* a love of the emotions in response to attraction. There is a strong element of friendship in this third word for love. The root means *to guard, to care for, to tend, to delight in some-*

one particularly, or to take pleasure in. It is a love resulting from a close relationship and shows concern and protectiveness for the one loved. It is the love of a close friend. Hence it is similar to the Greek *phileo.* Both *ra'eyah* and *phileo* would also fall under the wider umbrella of *ahavah* and *agapei,* for the latter would include the elements of *ra'eyah* and *phileo* yet are not limited to it.

In verse 2, the word translated "love" is *dod* which means sexual love. The root word means *to carouse, swing, rock, fondle, love, and to move by thrusts and pushes,* all of which have sexual connotations. This root refers to sexual activities in love, and all manifestations of sexual love.

Elsewhere, the word *dod* is found in passages which have obvious sexual connotations.

> Come, let us take our fill of love until the morning; Let us solace ourselves with loves. (Proverbs 7:18)

In Proverbs seven, Solomon is warning his son against giving in to a prostitute. Within that context, the word must refer to sexual activity. However, in Proverbs seven, sexual activity is being misused and therefore, in this case, it is sinful. But in the Song of Solomon there is the proper usage of sexual love portrayed as God had intended. For sex itself is not sin but can be used in a sinful way and for sinful purposes.

> Now when I passed by thee, and looked upon thee, behold, thy time was the time of love; and I spread my skirt over thee, and covered thy nakedness: yea, I sware unto thee, and entered into a covenant with thee, saith the Lord Jehovah, and thou becamest mine. (Ezekiel 16:8).

As the context makes clear, this too is a reference to sexual love. In this passage sexual love is seen in a positive light, whereas in the next it is seen in the negative side:

> And the Babylonians came to her into the bed of love, and they defiled her with their whoredom, and she was polluted with them, and her soul was alienated from them. (Ezekiel 23:17).

Hence, it is clear both from the root and from usage that this word *dod* refers to sexual love, and that it is used both in a good and evil sense. In the Song of Solomon it is used only in a good sense.

Thus Shulamit's opening line is a longing for their first sexual union to take place. While she is getting ready for the wedding feast, she is already longing to go beyond the feast looking forward to the bridal chamber itself. Thus her first desire "Let him kiss me" for his sexual love is better than wine is actually a desire for their first sexual union in order to consummate the marriage. Kissing here is used in the sense of foreplay in preparation for sexual love.

In verse three, the second reason for the desire is given: the fragrance and quality of his love. At the banquet not only will wine be present, but the entire palace will be sprinkled with perfume. Yet the fragrance of Solomon's love surpasses the fragrance of the royal palace. In fact, all the fragrances are surpassed by the very fragrance of his name alone. The "poured out oil" refers to an ointment which, having been taken out of its depository, is sprinkled far and wide. To Shulamit, Solomon's name is like this kind of ointment. In light of all this, it is no wonder that the virgins love him. The word "virgins" refers to young virgins of marriageable age, and no doubt many of them had the longing to become Solomon's choice before Shulamit was finally chosen to be the one.

In verse 4a Shulamit expresses a second desire "Draw me." The Hebrew word implies a gentle drawing of love towards itself. It is so used in Jeremiah 31:3:

> Jehovah appeared of old unto me, saying, Yea, I have loved thee with an everlasting love: therefore with loving kindness have I drawn thee.

This same sense of gentle drawing of love is also found in Hosea 11:4:

> I drew them with cords of a man, with bands of love; and I was to them as they that lift up the yoke on their jaws; and I laid food before them.

The second desire then is to be drawn, pulled, and enveloped by love itself. While the first desire was for sexual love, this second is for the emotional expression of love which gives sexual love its meaning. The practice of sexual love apart from the emotion and will of love (*ahavah*) reduces it to lust. Proper sexual love in the Scriptures is a high state to be practiced only in the context of the entire biblical concept of love.

In answer to the two desires comes the refrain: "The king has brought me into his chamber."

This brings a response from the Daughters of Jerusalem found in 1:4b:

> We will be glad and rejoice in you,
>   We will bring to remembrance your love more than wine,
> Uprightly do they love you.

The word translated "glad" means *conduct showing delight* while the word translated "rejoice" means *to be of a joyful and bright disposition.* The object of all this delight is found in the words "in you." It expresses the object *on account of* whom and *in* whom one has joy. So the Daughters of Jerusalem will be glad and rejoice because of Shulamit; there will be no jealousy here. Furthermore, they will praise her, which is what is implied in "bringing to remembrance." It is to bring to remembrance frequently in the way of praise (cf. Psalm 45:17). Thus, in Shulamit's enjoyment of sexual love, the Daughters of Jerusalem will rejoice with her and because of her.

In the English text the word "love" appears twice, but in the Hebrew text two different words are used. In the line, "we will bring to remembrance your love more than wine," it is *dod* that is used which refers to sexual love. If admitted to the closest presence of the king, the imaginary chorus will praise sexual love more than wine.

In the line "uprightly do they love you," it is *ahavah* that is used. The virgins of the palace love the royal couple from a right heart. "Right" here is not a righteousness of motive but of word, thought and deed.

In verses 5-6 Shulamit speaks again to the Daughters of Jerusalem:

(5)   I am black but lovely,
         Daughters of Jerusalem;
    As the tents of Kedar,
    As the tent-curtains of Solomon.

(6)   Do not look at me
         That I am blackish,
         That the sun scorched me;
    The sons of my mother were incensed against me,
         They placed me as a keeper of vineyards;
         My vineyard, even mine, I have not kept.

The praise having just emanated from the Daughters of Jerusalem makes Shulamit conscious of her swarthy complexion. Shulamit expresses humility balanced by a recognition of beauty nonetheless.

The expressions of humility begin with "I am black." The word translated "black" is used of skin, hair, and color, but never of race. The idea is not that she is black naturally but of becoming and growing dark. It is not pitch-black, but deep nevertheless. But the statement of humility is balanced with "but beautiful" or better "becoming beautiful." Thus the expression of humility is without abjectivity.

The contrast of "I am black - - - - - but lovely" is followed by a second contrast "the tents of Kedar - - - - - the tent curtains of Solomon." The "tents of Kedar" answers to "I am black" and refers to the black tents of the Bedouins. These were generally made of black goat skins and hair. The "tent curtains" answers to "but lovely" referring to Solomon's pleasure tent. The word is used for the sides of a tent in Isaiah 54:2, Jeremiah 4:20, 10:20, 49:29, and Habakkuk 3:7. It is used of the tabernacle in the wilderness in Exodus 26-27 and of the tabernacle of Zion in II Samuel 7:2 and I Chronicles 17:1.

Shulamit thus recognizes both her shortcomings and her strengths. In verse 6 she explains how she got that way. She states she is "blackish." This is a slightly different word than that found in the previous verse and means that which is black here and there. Her brothers forced her to work in the family vineyards which, unlike orchards, provide very little shade. Thus she was scorched with the sun on the exposed parts of her body, and this is the reason for her complexion. But her very own vineyard, a reference to her own feminine beauty and charms, she did not keep but let it become blackish here and there, in a spotty way.

So while she did well in keeping the family vineyards, she failed to take care of her own physical appearance. Yet in spite of that physical appearance, and in spite of the contrast with the fair-skinned palace girls, it was with Shulamit that Solomon fell in love, and it was her that he wanted.

This fact reminds Shulamit of an incident during courtship. Solomon the king began courting her posing as a simple shepherd withholding his true identity. In 1:7 she recalls her unsuccessful attempts to discover the strange shepherd's identity:

> Tell me, you who my soul loves,
>> Where do you shepherd,
>> Where do you cause it to rest at noon,
> For why should I be as a veiled one
>> By the flocks of your friends?

The question is: "Where can I find you at work?" He had won her love, but he was still silent concerning himself. Why should she go around looking for him as a veiled woman looking for a man thus creating the wrong impression. "Veiled one" refers to the practice of a prostitute, as is seen in Genesis 38:14-15. She seeks to know exactly where he can be found so that it will not appear that she is a prostitute walking aimlessly around looking for a male consort.

The answer comes from the Daughters of Jerusalem in 1:8:

> If you yourself do not know
>> Most beautiful of women,
> Go forth by the footsteps of the flock
>> And shepherd your kids by the tent of the shepherd.

Eventually the true identity of the shepherd is revealed. Having found out that it was Solomon, she must choose whether or not to marry Solomon and follow his footsteps to his tent, which now is obviously the royal palace in Jerusalem. It is a conflict that must be resolved. With this instruction and admonition from the Daughters of Jerusalem, the first reflection comes to an end.

Summary — In the first reflection (1:2-8) Shulamit is in the palace getting ready for the wedding banquet and the wedding night to follow. While doing so she expresses desires to the imaginary Daughters of Jerusalem. Her first desire is for him to kiss her as the prelude to their first night together. There are two reasons for this. First, his sexual love is better than wine, and secondly, his love is a sweet fragrance. She is looking forward in great anticipation to their first night together. Her second desire is for him to draw her to himself. The answer to her two desires comes when the king brings her into his chambers (1:2-4a).

This brings on a response from the Daughters of Jerusalem who declare that they are rejoicing and are glad because of Shulamit. If they were admitted to the closest presence of the king, they would praise sexual love more than wine. It is right that the royal couple is loved in word, thought, and deed (1:4b).

Shulamit is still conscious of her swarthy appearance, but this is balanced with the knowledge that Solomon did pick her out from among all other women. She is black but beautiful. Her blackness may look like the black goat skins of Bedouin tents, but there is beauty there, even the beauty of the curtains of Solomon's pleasure tent (1:5). She then explains the reason for her complexion. Her brothers forced her to work in the vineyards which provided little shade, and so her skin was scorched. So while she did well in keeping the vineyards, she failed in developing her own feminine charms and physical appearance (1:6).

She then begins to reminisce about the courtship days when Solomon, posing as a simple shepherd, began courting her without revealing his true identity. He had won her love but was still silent concerning himself (1:7). The first reflection ends with a response from the Daughters of Jerusalem regarding her need to resolve the conflict of her love for him (1:8).

Application — A number of principles can be learned from this first reflection by way of application.

First, Shulamit had developed a proper attitude toward sex and looked forward to their first sexual union with eager anticipation. In too many marriages and in too many young Christians entering marriage, there exists a wrong attitude toward sex. Some look at it as a necessary evil for procreation and the negative attitude is already there. The source of this attitude may have been instilled by well meaning parents, church, or the excesses of modern pornography. Regardless of the reason, a wrong attitude toward sex will eventually create marital tension. A proper attitude toward sex must include several aspects. First, it is the means by which God has chosen to procreate the race (Genesis 1:28). To multiply and to fill the earth with human beings can only be accomplished by the sex act. A second aspect is that it is by means of the sex act that a man and a woman truly become one whether it is within marriage as in Genesis 2:23-25:

> And the man said, This is now bone of my bones, and flesh of my flesh: she shall be called Woman, because she was taken out of Man. Therefore shall a man leave his father and his mother, and shall cleave unto his wife; and they shall be one flesh. And they were both naked, the man and his wife, and were not ashamed.

Or outside of marriage as in I Corinthians 6:16:

Or know ye not that he that is joined to a harlot is one body? for, the twain, saith he, shall become one flesh.

In the biblical ideal oneness is to be expressed only within the marriage bond. This is emphasized by Christ in Matthew 19:4-6:

And he answered and said, Have ye not read, that he who made them from the beginning made them male and female, and said, For this cause shall a man leave his father and mother, and shall cleave to his wife; and the two shall become one flesh? So that they are no more two, but one flesh. What therefore God hath joined together, let not man put asunder.

A third aspect is the fact that sex is to be used for pleasure, and it is this aspect that is emphasized throughout the Song of Solomon. Physical pleasure derived from sex must not be viewed as "dirty" or sinful but as a very beautiful thing to be looked forward to.

A second application from this passage is that sexual love must only be practiced within the entire concept of the *ahavah* or *agapei* love. There must first be a commitment of the will to love the person, and such a commitment can only be made by the marriage vow. A sexual relationship must be the physical outworking of the *ahavah* love of commitment. Without that kind of love, sex becomes merely lust, setting out to satisfy self without concern for the mate. However, if sex is viewed as a physical expression of the entire biblical concept of love, then it elevates sex to a very beautiful thing. For this very reason, sex must be practiced only within the marriage bond.

A third application can be derived from Shulamit's proper evaluation of herself. She recognized her own strengths and short-comings and kept them in balance. A common detriment to marriage that comes out in counseling sessions is an imbalance of one's evaluation of oneself at the time of marriage. One extreme is "I could have gotten anyone I wanted," and the other is "Boy, am I lucky to have found someone willing to marry me!" These attitudes only bring feelings of superiority or inferiority into the marriage relationship. It results in both competition and deflation within the marriage relationship. It is neither wrong to recognize one's strong points nor demeaning to recognize one's weak points. Every person has both, and so it will be for the rest of one's life. But these things must be kept in their proper balance. Recognition must be given to the fact that the mate "chose me in spite of my shortcomings because I was loved as a person."

A fourth application comes out of the one thing Shulamit would have done over again had she had the chance. She regretted that she did not take better care of her physical appearance. She now intends to correct that problem, but it is too late to do anything about her swarthy complexion. There is no reason for a Christian to look like a "plain-Jane" or a "plain-Joe." We should always strive to look our very best for our mate. It is a natural thing to do during courtship, but it should be more true after marriage than before marriage. But it is right here that things often break down. During courtship, every effort is made to look our best. After the honeymoon and after the first year or two, these efforts often break down until the only time the mate tries to look good is when they go out. However, special care for one's physical appearance should be more of a habit after marriage than before, and for the purpose of impressing the mate. So just as Shulamit commits herself to improve her physical appearance after marriage, so should the Christian couple.

A fifth application comes from the decision that Shulamit had to make between choosing to remain home in the country or choosing to make the break with her past, her home, and all that that includes, to be entirely united with her mate. That is the point of the principle of leaving and cleaving in Genesis 2:23-24. Once we have made the commitment of the marriage bond, the break with our home should be complete. Our future lies with the future of our mate. There is no such thing as separate ministries or callings, for the calling of the wife is the calling of the husband. The woman must commit herself to go wherever her mate may be and that is her new position from which she is not to look back. Many "in-law" problems could be resolved by the application of this very principle.

Reflection Two: At The Wedding Feast

1:9-14

In the second reflection Solomon and Shulamit are seen as reclining at the wedding feast and mutually praising each other's beauty. The second reflection begins with Solomon addressing Shulamit in 1:9-11:

(9)   To the mares among the chariots of Pharoah
          I have compared you, my love!
(10)   Beautiful are your chains in ornaments,
          Your neck with strings of jewels,
(11)   Ornaments of gold we will make for you
          With studs of silver.

While in today's world one would not compare his wife to a horse in a complimentary fashion, things were different in the ancient world. The fact that Solomon was speaking these words is significant for it is known that he was a great lover of horses (cf. I Kings 4:26, 10:26). Furthermore, many of his horses came from Egypt (I Kings 10:28-29), hence the reference to Pharoah's mares. Since the royal horses were well ornamented, verses 10-11 continue to describe the ornamental beauty of Shulamit in comparison to the royal steeds. (Some real positive features of horses are described in Job 39:19-25).

The word translated "love" in verse 9 is the word *ra'eyah,* which means *a close personal friend.*

Shulamit responds next in 1:12-14:

(12) While the king was at his banquet table,
           My nard gave off its fragrance;
(13) A bundle of myrrh is my love to me
           Which lies between my breasts,
(14) A cluster of copher is my love to me
           In the vineyards of Ein Gedi.

Whereas Solomon compared Shulamit to the loveliest of mares and to jewels, she compares him to the finest spices.

In verse 12 Shulamit speaks of her nard giving off its fragrance while they were reclining at the banquet table. Nard came from a fragrant plant of that name from India. It had a sweet smell and was very expensive. This is what Mary poured out on the feet of Jesus, and the fragrance filled the entire house with a sweet odor evoking a complaint from Judas of the wasted expense involved (Mark 14:3-5, John 12:3-5). It was also a spice used to arouse sexual passion, and it is in this sense that it is used here (cf. Isaiah 3:24, Esther 2:12).

In verse 13 there is an allusion to the ancient practice of women wearing a bundle of myrrh from a chain hanging around their necks giving off a pleasant smell counter-acting body odor. Myrrh too comes from a fragrant substance of a plant from India, and in the Scriptures it is used for various purposes. In Psalm 45:8 it is used for garments and in Esther 2:12 for the body. Throughout the book of Proverbs it is used in terms of sexual passion (e.g. Proverbs 7:17). Since Solomon authored both the Proverbs and the Song of Solomon, it would appear that this is the sense here. Solomon is described as that bundle of myrrh giving off a pleasant fragrance.

In verse 14 Solomon is further described as a cluster of copher. The copher was the cypress or henna flower, a plant with fragrant yellow and white flowers.

Thus during the wedding banquet which comes between the wedding ceremony and the wedding night, Solomon and Shulamit describe each other's beauty and satisfaction with each other.

Summary — Reflection two (1:9-14) is at the banquet table following the marriage ceremony and before the wedding night. There Solomon and Shulamit are reclining at the wedding feast and mutually praise each other's beauty. First Solomon compares her beauty to fine mares and expensive jewels (1:9-11) while Shulamit compares Solomon to the finest of spices (1:12-14).

Application — Two points by way of application can be deduced from this reflection. First is the importance of verbalizing to your mate your appreciation of your mate. This may involve the mate's physical beauty, the little things the mate does or whatever. It should never be simply assumed that your mate knows he or she is being appreciated. It must be verbalized, for only then will there be real assurance. It is a good practice for the husband to tell his wife once a day that he loves her.

A second application is the physical aspect. Both Solomon and Shulamit wore perfume so as to appear more pleasant to each other and to arouse each other for the act of love. In the same way a married couple should make it a practice to apply those perfumes and spices that appear pleasing to the mate. To make use of "Avon calling" need not be looked upon as an unnecessary extravagance. In connection with this it should be kept in mind that body odor and sweat are rarely a turn on. Perfumes may hide a lot but not an unclean body. Anyone desiring a satisfying sexual response from their mate should be alert to body cleanliness.

Reflection Three: In The Bridal Chamber

1:15–2:7

With the third reflection, the newly married couple move into the wedding chamber and spend their first night together. Here their first sexual union is erotically and beautifully described.

This begins with Solomon addressing Shulamit in 1:15:

> Behold you are beautiful my love,
>> Behold you are beautiful:
>> Your eyes are as doves.

Using *ra'eyah* for love, Solomon initiates the discourse of the wedding night by describing his infatuation with her beauty, especially as centered around her eyes.

Shulamit responds in 1:16–2:1:

> (16)   Behold, you are beautiful my love,
>> Yea, pleasant.
>> Yea, our couch is luxuriously green.
> (17)   The beams of our house are cedar,
>> Our rafters are cypresses.
> (1)   I am the autumn crocus of the Sharon,
>> The lily of the valley.

Shulamit responds to Solomon by describing the beauty she sees before those eyes (vs. 16a). She then proceeds (vs. 16b-17) to describe the beauty of the bridal chamber that Solomon constructed for the occasion. The cedars and cypresses are not native to Jerusalem but come from the north in Galilee, the area of Shulamit's home. Solomon had this kind of wood brought down, and he structured the bridal chamber to be like and to remind her of her home. Solomon created an atmosphere that would give it a sense of being a world apart; a world unique and all their own to be enjoyed by themselves alone.

Seeing the trouble Solomon had gone to to create the special effects, she again feels her sense of unworthiness and compares herself to a simple country flower, an autumn crocus (2:1) common in the Plain of Sharon (cf. Isaiah 35:1) and to a common lily found in the valleys of Israel.

But Solomon interrupts her comparison in 2:2:

> As a lily among thorns
>   So is my love among the daughters.

A common country flower perhaps, but one that surpasses everything around it. The word translated "thorns" is not the thorn of a flower stem such as the rose, but refers to the thorn plant or thorn bushes which are plentiful (cf. II Kings 14:9). So Solomon interrupts to respond — a simple common flower? Yes! But in that very simplicity of gentleness and innocence and beauty, Shulamit surpasses all the women just as the lily of the valley surpasses the thorn bushes all around it.

Again Shulamit speaks and in 2:3-6, she begins to describe their first sexual union:

> (3)   As the apple tree is among the trees of the forest
>   So is my love among the sons:
>   In his shade I took delight, and I sat down,
>   And his fruit was sweet to my taste.
> (4)   He brought me into the house of wine,
>   His banner over me is love.
> (5)   Sustain me with raisin cakes!
>   Refresh me with apples!
>   For I am love sick!
> (6)   His left hand is under my head,
>   And his right hand embraces me.

These verses describe in some detail the erotic pleasures of the wedding night by the use of erotic symbols common in ancient literature. Due to the sensitivities of many of God's people, it is not possible to detail the sexual acts implied in the Hebrew text lest we unnecessarily cause offense. Hence we will limit ourselves to basic descriptions.

Verse three describes the beginning of the sexual union by foreplay until sexual passion is aroused. Apples in the ancient world were erotic symbols, and this is the usage here.*

In verse four sexual passion rises because of the foreplay in the previous verse until they become delirious with it. This is the meaning of the expression "house of wine."

---

* Some commentators have viewed the last two lines of verse three as a reference to oral sex being performed by the bride.

In verse five the passion has reached the stage where it requires satisfaction through the sexual act itself. Both apples and raisin cakes were symbols of sexual passions. Hence she calls for these to satisfy the passion. So in essence, having been aroused through foreplay, she now seeks satisfaction by the sexual act itself. This is the sense of her statement "I am lovesick."

The answer to her request comes in verse six with the first sexual act as Solomon embraces his wife and takes her to himself and the marriage is consummated. They have become one. This answers her request for satisfaction.

This experience gives rise to Shulamit's admonition in 2:7:

> I adjure you,
>> O Daughters of Jerusalem,
>> By the gazelles or by the hinds of the field,
> That you do not arouse or stir up love
>> Until it is pleased.

The word "arouse" means *to excite the passions,* and "pleased" means *to satisfy* or *to fulfill.* Because of her experiences in verses 5-6, she admonishes that sexual passions must never be aroused unless they can also be satisfied or fulfilled; otherwise they will lead to frustration. Sexual passion must be handled with utmost care and should not be aroused before its proper time.

Summary — Reflection three (1:15–2:7) takes place in the bridal chamber where their first night of sexual love begins. The details are erotic, specific, but tasteful. It begins with Solomon declaring the beauty of Shulamit (1:15). Then Shulamit declares him to be the same and then begins to describe their bridal chamber which he had built especially for her to remind her most of home and where they had courted (1:16-17). She then compares herself to a common country flower (2:1), but Solomon disagrees and compares her to a lily that surpasses the thorn, for she surpasses all other women (2:2).

The first sexual union now takes place with foreplay as Shulamit takes the initiative (2:3). The increase of sexual passion that follows is described as reaching such heights as to demand satisfaction (2:4-5). Solomon responds by making love to her for the first time (2:6).

This reflection ends with Shulamit admonishing the Daughters of Jerusalem that sexual passion must never be aroused unless there can be satisfaction (2:7). Otherwise, this may lead to frustration. This is her conclusion based on her experience of the wedding night.

Application — The importance of verbalizing what you think to your mate is the first application from this reflection, and so re-emphasizes the lesson learned earlier. Both Solomon and Shulamit verbalized what they liked about each other and each other's beauty. Even as Shulamit again points out her shortcomings, Solomon does not deny that they exist but verbalizes to her how these very shortcomings make her unique in his eyes. But the stress is again the importance of verbalizing feelings and appreciations.

The second application concerns the bedroom. The bedroom occupied by the husband and wife should be looked upon as someplace special where sexual union takes place. The very decor of the bedroom should be such that just being there would stimulate romantic thoughts. The bedroom should not be characterized by clothes strewn all over the place, the dressers piled up with a bunch of junk. They make closets for things like that. Rather, the bedroom should be kept neat with an atmosphere that is extra special, for that is the only room that serves as the private domain of the husband and wife. This can be accomplished through the use of colored and/or hanging lights, fancy drapes, candles, a special bedspread, and other ways in which a couple can put their imagination to good use. But the key is to look upon the bedroom as an extra special place of rendezvous.

A third application emphasizes the importance of foreplay in preparation for sexual intercourse. This is an area that can only be learned by experience with each other after marriage. Proper sexual intercourse is an act that can only be developed by two people working and learning together and from each other. But every effort should be made to learn proper foreplay. Each mate will need to verbalize what pleases and arouses him or her to sexual passion so that both mates are fully ready for sexual intercourse. The husband will need to spend more time on this aspect since men are usually far more easily aroused than women. The wife should teach her husband where to caress and touch her in order to please her most. The husband should learn to control himself and wait until his wife is fully ready for intercourse before entering into the act. As was stated earlier, this is something that must be learned mutually, and each mate teaches the other.

Finally, there is the importance of the proper timing for sexual arousal. Passion in the mate must not be aroused unless it can also be satisfied lest it leave the mate frustrated. The act of teasing the mate to arousal and then cutting it off must not occur in the biblical use of sexual relations. Any mate that begins to sexually arouse his or her mate should do so with the intention of satisfying the arousal. Otherwise the result is frustration and leads to marital tension.

CHAPTER TWO

THE SECOND IDYLL: THE COURTSHIP PERIOD REFLECTIONS
2:8–3:5

The second idyll contains two reflections which occur during the time of courtship. Chronologically, these events occur before those of the first idyll. The previous idyll spoke of the marriage feast and the wedding night. This idyll explains how it all came about.

Reflection Four: A Springtime Visit
2:8-17

In this reflection Shulamit thinks back on her courtship days and remembers a springtime visit paid by Solomon to her home in Galilee, and how some pre-marital problems were solved so as to assure a better marriage later.

The fourth reflection begins with Shulamit describing Solomon's approach to her as he comes through the gate and peers at her through the windows in 2:8-9:

(8)   The voice of my beloved!
            Behold he comes,
        Leaping upon the mountains,
            Bounding on the hills.
(9)   My beloved is likened to a gazelle
            Or a young one among the harts.
        Behold he stands behind our wall;
            He is looking through the windows,
            He peers through the lattices.

"The voice of my beloved" is an interjectional clause and should be taken as the call of the approaching lover. He is calling for her as he is approaching. The content of that call will be described by Shulamit in verses 10-14. Depicting his desire to see the one he loves after a long winter's separation, Solomon is seen as springing and bounding with speed in eagerness to get to Shulamit's home. He is seen as coming with the speed of a gazelle as his eyes seek for his unforgotten one. Gazelles and harts climb mountains and leap over hills with ease and grace, and so does Solomon her beloved.

The word translated "wall" refers to the wall of the house itself rather than the outer wall surrounding the house, as this would require a different Hebrew word. The picture then is that Shulamit is within the house. Solomon, having leaped and bounded over the hills, now stands behind the wall outside and looks in through the window. The word translated "looking" means *to look by fixation for reflection and meditation.* The word translated "peers" means *to peep or to twinkle,* a reference to the quick darting and glances of the eye. It is a reference to the gleam of the eye. So while Solomon is trying to see his love through the window, he looks at one time through this window and then through another in order that he might see her. Once having seen her, he feasts his eyes on her and fixes them on her to reflect and to meditate over her.

Shulamit, having described Solomon's anxious approach to her home, now describes the words with which he called her in 2:10-14:

(10) My love answered and said to me,
      Rise thee up my love,
      My beautiful one,
  And go thee forth.
(11) For behold the winter is past,
  The rain is over and it is gone.
(12) The flowers have appeared in the land;
      The time of singing has arrived,
      And the voice of the turtledove is heard in our land.
(13) The fig tree ripens her figs,
      And the vines are in blossom;
      They give fragrance.
  Rise thee up my love,
      My beautiful one,
  And go thee forth.
(14) My dove
      In the clefts of the rock,
      In the hiding place of the cliff;
  Let me see your countenance,
  Let me hear your voice;
      Because your voice is sweet,
      And your countenances are beautiful.

In verse 10, Solomon comes to the country again after a long winter. Shulamit sees him, and he invites her to enjoy the spring with him. He calls upon her to rise from her stupor and to go out with him. Though Solomon has come north to take care of his fields in the Galilee, he desires to be with her for now and let his business lay.

In verses 11-13a he points to all the evidence of spring having arrived: the rains have ceased, the flowers have appeared, and birds have been heard to sing. Furthermore, the voice of the turtledove is heard. The turtledove is not so much a singing bird as it is a bird of passage, a migratory bird. The fact that its voice is now heard is clear evidence that spring has also arrived. Finally, the figs are ripening and the vines are in blossom giving off a sweet fragrance. Spring is in the air.

Having described the coming of spring, Solomon again urges Shulamit to rise from the winter's night and to go and walk with him through the spring (vs. 13b). Solomon and Shulamit are now ready for the fruition of their mutual love, for the long winter's separation did not chill their love for one another.

Solomon's pleading concludes with verse 14. Shulamit remaining in her house would be like a dove or a wood-pigeon that hides in the clefts of the rocks and other strong rocky places (cf. Jeremiah 48:28), thereby making itself inaccessible for it is in a secure hiding place. Solomon pleads for Shulamit to come out of her hiding place and make herself accessible to him. He wants to see her countenance or form because of its beauty. In Hebrew the word translated "countenance" is in the plural number, which in this case must be taken as a plural of amplification. Solomon wants to see her because of the fulness of her beauty and the overpowering impression she makes on him. Furthermore, he wants to hear her voice because of its sweetness.

Shulamit, in response to Solomon's call, now goes forward, and as they walk Shulamit speaks the words of 2:15-17:

(15)   Catch for us foxes,
            Little foxes,
            The spoilers of the vineyards.
(16)   My lover is mine and I am his,
            The shepherd among the lilies.
(17)   Until the day cools
            And the shadows flee away,
      Turn my love
            And be thou like a gazelle,
            Or a young one of the harts,
      Upon the mountains of separation.

In response to Solomon's call, Shulamit comes out and they begin to take a walk into the springtime. As they walk Shulamit notices the problems caused by little foxes in the vineyards. In verse 15 this fact begins to suggest to Shulamit the necessity of working out little problems that would hinder love or create tension later.

Little foxes burrow holes through the earth and this loosens the soil so that the growth and prosperity of the vine suffers. Foxes were proverbial destroyers and appear as such in Nehemiah 4:3, Lamentations 15:18 and Ezekiel 14:4. In this context these foxes are all great and little enemies which threaten, gnaw at and destroy love in blossom, before it ripens into full enjoyment. Thus Shulamit states that their love will indeed celebrate the new spring and that their love like the vineyards is indeed in blossom. But first she wishes everything removed or rendered harmless that would destroy the peace of love. Hence, "Catch the little foxes!"

But what exactly are these foxes she has reference to? This can be deduced from the next two verses. Verse 16 begins with a declaration that each belongs to the other — "I am yours and you are mine." The object of her love is Solomon the shepherd who has many holdings in land and sheep near her country home. He has business which must be attended to. But she is fully confident of their love remaining true to each other.

She then states "He shepherds among the lilies." She pictures him as a shepherd who during the day is feeding his flock and so is away from her. Solomon has business to attend to, and unless she allows him to attend to it, it will remain on his mind while he is spending time with her. She is confident that she and Solomon belong together, but he must tend to his business while it is day. So she sends him away to finish his duty. She allows him to do his work rather than selfishly hanging on to him. She does this in confidence knowing that their time will come when he can give her his undivided attention.

And so one of those little foxes has been caught. She will have Solomon complete his business. Then in the evening he is to return, when they can be together without the need of thinking about other matters. And so in verse 17 she bids him to return to her when the day cools, that is, in the time of the evening breezes. He is to return to her when the "shadows flee away," for as the sun goes down the shadows get longer until they disappear. This is when he is to return to her.

But when he returns, he is to do it with the same speed and anxiousness as he had in coming to her earlier. He is to skip and bounce over the "mountains of separation," that is, over the mountains and hills that separate Solomon from Shulamit. The peaks are to be a base from which he is to spring from one to another until he arrives to her again.

Solomon had invited Shulamit to enjoy the springtime with him. However, he has affairs to take care of during the day, and they do not have the time to wander together by themselves. So now she asks him to go and finish his work and then make haste at evening to come back to her. Then they will spend time together as he promised her. She will not claim him for herself until he has accomplished all his work. But when he returns to her in the evening, she will rejoice if he becomes her guide through the newborn spring. By letting him complete his work and thus clear it from his mind, she catches one little fox and renders it harmless.

By arranging time when they could be completely by themselves without outside interference, they catch another fox.

A third fox is caught by Solomon leaving his work at work and not bringing it home with him.

Summary — In reflection four (2:8-17) Shulamit reflects on a springtime visit Solomon made to her home. Shulamit describes his approach and call to her as he comes through the gate to the house where he peers at her through the window (2:8-9). Shulamit then relates the words of Solomon as he calls her in loving words. Spring is here and nature is coming to life as should their love (2:10-14).

As they walk, Shulamit notices the damage done to the vineyards by the little foxes. This suggests to Shulamit the necessity of working out the little problems between themselves before they enter into marriage. So before the love can come to fruition in marriage, she wants everything removed that might prove harmful. That is, to render harmless things that would disturb the peace of love. These little foxes represent all great and little things in adverse or even normal circumstances which threaten to gnaw at and destroy love in blossom before it ripens into full enjoyment (2:15).

One of these little foxes is to selfishly hang on to him and not let him complete his work. So she sends Solomon away in order that his business can be completed, while remaining confident in their mutual love. She allows him to do his work rather than to selfishly hang on. In this way she has rendered harmless one of the little foxes which can destroy their love by destroying his work (2:16). She can send him away in confidence knowing he will return to her in the evening when all of his time will be hers. She has caught one of the little foxes (2:17).

Application — Couples in courtship often recognize that certain problems exist but take the attitude of "We can work these things out after we are married." But after marriage, a whole new set of problems become apparent adding to those brought into the marriage to begin with. The end product is an accumulation of marital tensions. It is unavoidable that problems will arise both before and after marriage. Some problems cannot arise until the husband and wife actually start living together and develop new areas of relationships. But problems that become apparent and obvious before marriage should not be set aside to be dealt with after marriage. These should be worked out either by mutually talking things out in a very frank manner or by going to a Christian marriage counselor. But the problems must not be allowed to sit and ferment. "Little foxes" must be caught early whenever they can be in order to lessen the damage.

The second application is for the wife to see the importance of letting her husband finish his work and not to keep interfering by demanding attention so that his work suffers. A husband that sees his work suffering is apt to bring that tension into his relationship with his wife. Therefore, it is necessary for the wife to allow the husband to finish his work so that it can be out of his mind.

The third application applies to the other side of the coin. When the work day is over with, the husband should not bring his work home with him. This will be harder for those in the self-employed category, and this includes the minister. The tendency is to bring unfinished papers from the office to the home and work on them there. There will be occasions when this is absolutely necessary because of deadlines that must be met, but it must never be allowed to become a regular practice. The work should be left at work. Even when the office happens to be in one's home, it should stay in that office and not be brought to the dinner table or bedroom. The principle is to leave it there, and this involves the state of mind just as much as the geographical change.

The fourth application is a natural outworking of the second and third. The time a couple spends with each other should be totally theirs with undivided attention. This will be a natural result if on one hand the wife allows her husband to finish his business, while on the other hand he leaves his business at his place of work. The wife should schedule her activities in such a way as to be free when her mate is free. This is a mutual effort. Now both are ready for each other and so should spend their time with undivided attention to each other. Sharing time together builds the relationship while the lack of it erodes what is built.

Reflection Five: Dreams of Separation

3:1-5

After Solomon leaves, Shulamit remembers a recurring dream during the winter months in which she is separated from him and cannot find him, as recorded in 3:1-4:

(1)   Upon my bed night after night,
           I sought whom my soul loved;
           I sought him,
           But I did not find him.
(2)   I will rise up,
           And I will go around the city,
           In the markets and in the streets,
       I will seek him whom my soul loves.
           I sought him,
           But I did not find him.
(3)   The watchmen
           That go around the city
           Found me:
       Did you see whom my soul loves?
(4)   Scarcely had I passed from them
           When I found whom my soul loves,
       I seized him,
           And did not let him go,
       Until I brought him into the house of my mother,
           And into the chambers of the one who gave me birth.

Now that Solomon has left for the day, she remembers the recurring dream of separation. The long winter's separation and its attendant longing had crept into her dreams and turned them into nightmares.

In verse one the Hebrew word translated "night" is found in the plural number, meaning that the dream came for a number of nights. She would be sleeping when a painful longing would seize her. Solomon had appeared to have forsaken her and withdrawn from her, and she was unable to recover him.

So in verse two she ran around the city streets in the thick of the night looking for him, but was still unable to find him.

When the watchmen found her in verse three, she asked them of his whereabouts.

No sooner had the question left her mouth that she saw him (vs. 4). She then seized him. The Hebrew implies that she held him fast until she brought him with gentle strength into her mother's house. The mother's house represents a place of security. Her mother's chambers may have represented something special to Shulamit, a place of intimacy, and bringing Solomon there suggests the deepness of her affections for him. Thus the dream ends happily with Solomon found again and by her side. But this dream began with a nightmare.

Shulamit is only describing her dream. The events of the dream did not really happen but were brought about by a real event: the winter's separation from Solomon. These were merely dreams recurring over and over again that troubled her sleep through the long winter of separation. But now the spring is here and Solomon has returned, and she hopes these dreams will cease.

The second idyll ends in 3:5 with the same words found in 2:7:

> I adjure you,
>   O Daughters of Jerusalem,
>   By the gazelles and by the hinds of the field,
> That you do not arouse or stir up love,
>   Until it is pleased.

The vision of the dream with its ending in the mother's chambers leads to ecstasy. That she had her love all to herself alone causes her to fall into a love ecstasy as that recorded in 2:7. Although the words in 3:5 are the same as those in 2:7, they each make a different point. In 2:7 the statement was made in the context of marriage. The point was that sexual passion should not be aroused unless it can also be satisfied, otherwise it will lead to frustration. In 3:5 it is in the context of courtship, where sexual passion should not be aroused lest it lead to fornication and sin. This passage teaches that pre-marital petting must not be practiced. Sexual union and satisfaction is permissible only within the marriage bond. Hence, any kind of foreplay that arouses sexual passion is not to be practiced outside the marriage bond, for it may lead to fornication.

God has such a high view of sex that He will not permit it to be cheapened by lust. Therefore, not even acts of foreplay are permitted. Sexual passion must be handled with utmost care and should not be aroused before its proper time.

Summary — In reflection five (3:1-5) Shulamit recalls a recurring dream in which she is separated from Solomon and cannot find him. The long winter of separation in the previous reflection created a longing, giving rise to these dreams. In her dreams she sees herself looking for him but unable to find him (3:1). She begins to walk around the city looking for him and is still not able to find him (3:2). She runs into the watchmen and asks them if they saw her beloved (3:3). In this dream there is no response from them. Just as she passes them, she finds him. Seizing him tightly, refusing to let him go, she hangs on to him until she has brought him into her mother's house (3:4). The reflection ends with the adjuration to the Daughters of Jerusalem against the arousal of sexual passion unless it can be satisfied (3:5). But this time, being in the context of courtship rather than marriage, this was intended to avoid fornication. The previous time, being in a context of marriage, it meant to avoid frustration.

Application — The one application is obvious. While within the marriage bond sexual passion must not be aroused unless it can also be satisfied lest it lead to frustration, outside the marriage bond it can lead to fornication. Any kind of activity that tends to arouse the passions must be avoided by the courting couple. Sex is a beautiful thing and the wedding should mark the climax of courtship and the commencement of sexual life together. It should not be spoiled by allowing the passion to reach the stage of the point of no return. Foreplay in the form of petting must not be practiced because this leads to sexual arousal that cannot at this time be satisfied.

CHAPTER THREE

THE THIRD IDYLL: MARITAL UNION REFLECTIONS
3:6–5:1

The third idyll is the connecting link between idylls one and two. The first idyll dealt with the wedding banquet followed by the wedding night. The second idyll described an earlier time of courtship. This idyll deals with the marital union as the wedding takes place and is followed once again by the wedding night.

Reflection Six: The Wedding Procession
3:6-11

In the ancient system of marriage, especially in the Jewish world, there were five distinct steps which were followed:

1. The Betrothal — the time when the arrangement for the marriage was contracted. The fourth reflection dealt with this aspect;

2. The Wedding Procession — this was accomplished when the groom went to the house of the bride to fetch her (e.g. Matthew 25:1, Psalm 45) or sent a wedding party to fetch her to his home in a festal procession, and he would go forth to meet her (e.g. I Maccabees 9:37-39). This is spoken of in this sixth reflection;

3. The Wedding Ceremony — in which the two are recognized to be husband and wife in a legal sense. This aspect underlies the first reflection and will also be found in the sixth reflection;

4. The Wedding Feast or Banquet — this follows the wedding ceremony and is found in the second reflection;

5. The Wedding Night — in which the married couple become one in the flesh through the first sexual union. This was dealt with in the third reflection and will be dealt with again in the seventh reflection.

In this sixth reflection there is a description of the elegant wedding procession sent by Solomon. In accordance with the second step of the marriage system, Solomon sent a wedding party from Jerusalem to Galilee to fetch Shulamit for the marriage ceremony in Jerusalem. In this reflection we see the wedding party returning towards Jerusalem with the bride already in their midst.

This entire section is sung by a chorus witnessing the procession.

The scene begins by recording a question from one of the people in the crowd watching the procession in 3:6:

> Who is this one coming up from the wilderness,
>> Like pillars of smoke perfumed of myrrh and frankincense
>> From all the scented powders of the merchants?

The question is asked by a member of the crowd. From the first line of the question we can determine where the wedding party is located. The fact that Shulamit is seen as "coming up" points to the fact that she is approaching Jerusalem. The fact that she is coming up from "the wilderness" or the desert tells us the route the procession took from Galilee. She came from the north via the Jordan Valley and is now approaching Jerusalem via the Jericho-Jerusalem road. Thus the bride has been fetched and, after a long march, is now on the outskirts of Jerusalem, and the people are wondering as to the identity of the procession.

The royal honors accorded to Shulamit are seen in Solomon's lavish expenditure of spices making smoke and fragrance, which signaled Shulamit's approach from afar. Myrrh was a component of the holy oil in Exodus 30:23-25, and frankincense was a component of the holy incense in Exodus 30:34-35. The burning of the incense caused columns of smoke which marked the procession before and after, and it was scented with fragrant powders brought by merchants from the exotic East. Indeed, Solomon treated his bride like the queen she already was to him.

Another person in the crowd answers the question in 3:7-8:

> (7) Behold the travel-couch of Solomon:
>> Sixty mighty men are around it
>> From the mighty men of Israel;
> (8) All of them are handlers of sword,
>> Expert in war;
>> Each one has his sword on his thigh,
>> Against fear in the nights.

These two verses identify the wedding procession. In the center of attention is the "travel-couch of Solomon." The travel-couch (Hebrew: *mitah*) was a special royal bed made for the occasion; it is the royal litter on which she travels. Thus she can travel in comfort by lying on the travel-couch which is carried by several men.

Next the protective escort is described. The wedding party consisted of sixty of the royal palace guard. These men were not just a figurehead royal body guard as that of the Swiss Guard in the Vatican, but men who were experienced in war and known for their fighting ability. So in addition to the royal honor as seen in the spices, Solomon took care to have his bride protected in order to avoid the situation of I Maccabees 9:37-41:

After this came word to Jonathan and Simon his brother, that the children of Jambri made a great marriage, and were bringing the bride from Nadabatha with a great train, as being the daughter of one of the great princes of Chanaan. Therefore they remembered John their brother, and went up, and hid themselves under the covert of the mountain: where they lifted up their eyes, and looked, and, behold, there was much ado and great carriage: and the bridegroom came forth, and his friends and brethren, to meet them with drums, and instruments of music, and many weapons. Then Jonathan and they that were with him rose up against them from the place where they lay in ambush, and made a slaughter of them in such sort, as many fell down dead, and the remnant fled into the mountain, and they took all their spoils. Thus was the marriage turned into mourning, and the noise of their melody into lamentation.

Next the reflection draws attention away from the travel-couch in the procession to the palace where the bridal bed awaits her in 3:9-10:

(9)   A bed of state King Solomon made for himself,
          From the trees of Lebanon:
(10) Its pillars are made of silver,
          Its support of gold,
          Its cushion of purple,
          Its interior adorned from love
              By the Daughters of Jerusalem.

This passage does not describe further the travel-couch (*mitah*), but rather the marriage bed (*apiryon*). The *apiryon* was a bed with a canopy, hence a bed of state. Shulamit is traveling on the *mitah*, the royal litter. But in the palace the *apiryon*, the marriage bed for the wedding night, awaits her.

A detailed description is given of this bed. The wood used was of the cedar tree blending it in with the rest of the decor found in the bridal chamber (1:17). While 1:17 described the bridal chamber, these verses (3:9-10) describe the wedding bed itself found in the bridal chamber. The pillars at the head of the bed were made of silver. The supports, its legs, were made of gold. The cushion on the divan which served as a seat or a couch was made of red purple. The interior, the covering which lay on the couch, was made of tapestry. Because of their love for the king, the Daughters of Jerusalem procurred a costly tapestry which they had spread over the red purple cushion.

This is the elaborate marriage bed awaiting Shulamit.

This reflection closes with an admonition to the Daughters of Jerusalem in 3:11:

Go ye forth and look ye,
    O Daughters of Jerusalem,
    At King Solomon,
With the crown with which his mother crowned him
    On the day of his wedding,
    And on the day of the gladness of his heart.

This verse encourages the Daughters of Jerusalem to follow after Solomon as he meets his bride for the wedding ceremony, and the wedding procession comes to an end. They are to look at Solomon with the crown on his head. This crown is not the royal crown of his kingship, but a wedding crown. The custom of the ancient world was to crown the groom with a crown on his wedding day. On his wedding day a groom was considered a king. Hence Solomon's crown is not the royal crown, but the wedding crown especially made for this occasion by his mother Bathsheba.*

At this point the wedding ceremony occurs. The Hebrew word for wedding, *hatunah,* is found in verse 11. The root is *hatan,* which means *to cut into, to press into, or to go into,* and points to the first intercourse as being the act in which marriage is truly consummated.

With this reflection the wedding procession has come to an end, and the wedding ceremony has taken place. The wedding banquet took place in reflections one and two. Now, as in reflection three, the following reflection again describes the wedding night.

Summary — Reflection six (3:6-11) describes the wedding procession as the bride is brought from her home in Galilee to Jerusalem for the wedding. As the people of Jerusalem look towards the wilderness, they see a procession and inquire as to the identity of the one coming whose approach is marked before and after by columns of smoke ascending from the burning of expensive incense: myrrh and frankincense (3:6). The answer is that this is the travel-couch of Solomon upon which Shulamit rides, and it is protected by sixty mighty men of Israel (3:7), all of whom are experienced fighters and are ready and on the alert to protect the bride (3:8). This body guard was sent by Solomon to fetch his bride to Jerusalem for the wedding ceremony.

But then attention is drawn away from the magnificent travel-couch of Solomon to the even more magnificent canopied bed that Solomon had constructed for the wedding night (3:9-10). This reflection ends with the Daughters of Jerusalem encouraged to go out to see Solomon's royal appearance on his wedding day, especially the crown provided by his mother Bathsheba for the occasion (3:11).

Application — The one application from this reflection concerns the bedroom again. In a previous application, it has been stressed how important it is to turn the bedroom into a special decor in general. This application concerns specifically the bed itself. It should be a bed that is special and romantic in its very nature. This could be done by imitating Solomon and saving up for a canopied bed. But there are other

---

* This practice was discontinued with the destruction of Jerusalem in 70 A.D. Today a wine glass is broken during a Jewish wedding ceremony to symbolize that destruction, for even on the occasion of a Jew's happiest day, the wedding day, Jerusalem must be remembered.

ways to romanticize the master bed, such as using silk or satin sheets, or using soft and decorated bedspreads. Here again the couple's imagination should be activated for the purpose of making the bed a very special place.

Reflection Seven: The Wedding Night

4:1–5:1

The aim of this reflection is to give a fuller detailed description of the wedding night already partially described in the third reflection. Whereas in the third reflection the primary concern was the effects of the wedding night on Shulamit, here in this seventh reflection the primary concern is on the effects on Solomon. It is Solomon who speaks the entire passage with the exception of 4:16 where Shulamit speaks. As in the third reflection, because of certain sensitivities on the part of many believers, some elements of the details described in the Hebrew will not be brought out in this exposition. We will explain the events in more general terms.

This reflection begins with Solomon praising the outward attributes of his wife, beginning with her head and working down in 4:1-5:

(1)   Behold you are beautiful my love,
            Behold you are beautiful;
        Your eyes are doves behind your veil;
        Your hair is as a flock of goats
            Reposed downwards from Mount Gilead.
(2)   Your teeth are like a flock of shorn sheep,
            Which come up from the washing;
        That all of them have twins,
            And a lost one there is not among them.
(3)   As a thread of scarlet are your lips,
            And your mouth is beautiful;
        As a piece of pomegranate are your temples,
            Behind your veil.
(4)   As the Tower of David
            Your neck is built in terraces;
        There one thousand shields are hung upon it,
            All the armor of the mighty men.
(5)   Your two breasts are two fawns,
            Twins of a gazelle,
            The ones feeding among the lilies.

Solomon starts out with a general description "You are beautiful my love, you are beautiful." Then he begins to speak of specific features regarding the outward beauty of his bride. Her eyes are like doves behind her veil. It was customary for the bride to be veiled on the wedding night (cf. Genesis 24:65). It was called a veil because it hid the bride's face. This accounts for Jacob's inability to recognize the fact that his wedding night was spent with Leah and not with Rachel (Genesis 29:21-30). But in the case of Shulamit, her eyes gleamed through the veil.

Her hair is compared to a flock of goats reposed on a hillside. In Israel the goats are mostly black. Shulamit's hair is described as a flock of black goats seemingly impaled on a steep slope of the mountain side giving the appearance of hanging down on the sides of the cliffs. This often presented a lovely view to an otherwise boring scene, for the slopes of Mount Gilead rising from the Jordan Valley are very bare with a brown-bronze color. This is how the locks of Shulamit's hair appear to Solomon as they hang over her shoulders.

While her hair is compared to goats, her teeth are compared to sheep. In Israel sheep are primarily white. Her teeth are compared to shorn sheep because of their smoothness, and to washed sheep on account of their whiteness. Her teeth are like twin sheep because the two rows of teeth match each other. Her teeth are like a mother sheep which has not lost any of her young, which means that Shulamit has all her teeth.

Her lips are a scarlet crimson red surrounding a beautiful mouth. The temples refer to the thin piece of skull and indented skin on the sides of her eyes. In the case of Shulamit, her temples are the color of pomegranates, a mixture of dark and pale red. It is a redness tempered with a ruby color.

Her neck is likened to the Tower of David. The tower was built in terraces surrounded by the shields of the royal guard.* Shulamit's neck was long and surrounded by ornaments giving the appearance of terraces.

Finally, coming to the breasts, he compares the bosom from which the breasts rise to a field covered with lilies where the twin-paired young gazelles feed. The latter reference is both to the breasts and the nipples of the breasts.

Solomon has thus described the seven-fold beauty of his bride (her eyes, hair, teeth, mouth, temples, neck, and breasts). This praise leads to further excitement, and he begins to look forward to their first intercourse in 4:6:

> Until the day will cool,
>> And the shadows flee away,
> I will get me to the mountain of myrrh,
>> And unto the hill of frankincense.

---

*   Shields were often hung on tower walls (Ezekiel 27:11, I Maccabees 4:57). Solomon made 200 golden targets and 300 golden shields, and they were put into the house of the Forest of Lebanon (I Kings 10:16) which served as the royal armory (Isaiah 22:8) and may have been also known as the Tower of David. These shields were later carried away by Pharoah Shishak at the time of Rehoboam, Solomon's son, who replaced them with brass shields for his bodyguard to use (I Kings 14:25-28, II Chronicles 12:9-11). It was given to the captain of the guard at the time of the ascension of Joash to the throne (II Kings 11:10, II Chronicles 23:9).

"The mountain of myrrh" and "hill of frankincense" refer to what is known in other literature as "the mount of venus." It is a reference to the female sexual organs centered in the area of the pubic hair which covers a small mount. Having surveyed erotically the beauties of his bride, he is anxious to enjoy her completely and to have their first intercourse together.

This excitement is further aroused as Solomon next exclaims the words of 4:7-9:

(7)   All of you is beautiful my love,
           And there is no blemish in you.
(8)   With me from Lebanon, my bride,
           With me from Lebanon you will come:
       Journey down from the top of Amana,
           From the top of Senir and Hermon,
       From the dens of lions,
           From the mountains of the leopards.
(9)   You have ravished my heart, my sister-bride,
           You have ravished my heart,
       With one of your glances,
           With one little chain on your neck.

In verse seven, having previously extolled the specific features of his bride, Solomon concludes that all of her shares the beauty. He is totally satisfied with his bride.

As his ecstasy over his bride is rising, he invites Shulamit to go with him to Lebanon (vs. 8), and then descend with him from the steep heights of the mountains for even more ecstatic experiences. The word translated "journey" has the secondary meaning of *to view* or *to go in order to view.* This verse is not giving the origin of Shulamit, for she is from Galilee. Rather, Solomon is asking his bride to travel with him in order to view some ecstatic sights.

In verse nine the word "bride" is used for the first time. The Hebrew word comes from a root which means *to pierce through* and carries the meaning of *that which is brought to completion* (cf. Ezekiel 27:4, 11). Putting the two concepts together, the Hebrew word used for "bride" refers to one who has reached the goal of her womanly calling, that of becoming a sexual partner to her husband thus perfectly completing herself and him.

Verse nine further describes Solomon's ecstasy as the very look of Shulamit begins to ravish Solomon toward sexual arousal.

Solomon now begins to initiate foreplay, and further describes the features of his bride in 4:10-11:

(10)   How beautiful is your love, my sister-bride.
            How better is your love than wine,
            And the smell of your oils than spices.
(11)   Your lips drip honeycomb, my bride;
            Honey and milk are under your tongue;
        And the smell of your garments,
            As the smell of Lebanon.

The word for love in verse 10 is *dod,* meaning sexual love. Thus at this point active foreplay begins whereas in the previous section Solomon was merely eyeing the beauties of his new wife. In these two verses he again describes the beauties of his new wife, but this time from a different perspective. Previously he used the Hebrew word *yaphu* translated "beautiful" (vs. 1), which describes her love relative to the impression she made on him visually. That description is found in verses 1-5. But now, using the word *tovu,* also translated "beautiful," he describes her love relative to his physical experience of her. Thus earlier he had praised her for her outward beauties which he saw *(yaphu),* but now he will extol the beauties of her love according to what he experiences in their first intercourse *(tovu).*

Verse 11 continues to point to the fact that this is a description based on experience and not on sight alone. Her lips are like virgin honey that flows of itself from the honeycomb. Previously (vs. 3) her lips were described as to their color in accordance with how they appeared to his sight. Now, however, as foreplay begins with the kissing of the lips, he is describing them according to his physical experiences with them. The senses of taste and smell are intricately involved.

Picking up from the "mount of venus," the pubic hair area of verse six, Solomon next centers his attention upon that area of Shulamit's body in 4:12-15:

(12)   A locked garden is my sister-bride,
        A locked spring,
        A fountain sealed.
(13)   Your shoots are an orchard of pomegranates
        With choice fruits,
        Camphire with nard plants.
(14)   Nard and saffron,
        Calamus and cinnamon,
        With all the trees of frankincense,
        Myrrh and aloes with all chief spices.
(15)   A fountain of gardens,
        A well of living waters,
        And streams from Lebanon.

In this passage Shulamit's female genitals are described in terms of a garden, not at all unusual in the literature of the ancient world. Shulamit's sexual organs are like a "locked garden," a garden with a fenced enclosure around it. She is also a "locked spring." A locked garden and a locked spring mean that no one has access to these things but the rightful owner. On the other hand, a "sealed fountain" is one that is shut up against all impurities. The point is that Shulamit is a virgin. As a locked garden and as a locked spring, only the rightful owner is to have access to her and open her. As a sealed fountain means no one else has ever had her, and hence she was kept from all the impurities of fornication. Solomon, the rightful owner, now desires sexual satisfaction with her and only by her will he be satisfied.

The sprouts of verse 13 and the living waters of verse 15 are things that sprout or spring from within. In verses 13b-14 there is given the figure of fragrant plants which were used for the purpose of sexual arousal and stimulation. Solomon is describing the lubricating secretions resulting from the foreplay and needed for intercourse. Concerning the nard and camphire, refer to comments found under 1:13. Saffron was obtained from the crocus in Israel and used as a condiment. Calamus was a plant with a reed-like stem and tawny color imported from India. Cinnamon came from the East Indies, and aloes from India. Thus the foreplay has reached a stage of excitement where the lubricating juices have begun to flow in the preparation for intercourse.

It is at this point that Shulamit speaks in 4:16:

> Awake thou North (wind)!
> And come thou South (wind)!
> Cause my garden to breathe out its fragrance,
> Let its spices be wafted about;
> Let my love come into his garden,
> And let him eat its choice fruits.

The west wind brings rain (I Kings 18:44-45) and the east wind is hot and withering (Genesis 41:23, Job 27:27). But the north wind clears the air with cool breezes (Job 37:21-22) and the south wind brings warmness (Job 37:17). Thus the north and south winds promote growth if they come and interchange at proper times. As a result the entire garden becomes a sea of incense and fragrance, and the garden itself blows out its odor with fragrant plants. And so, foreplay administered properly and timely causes Shulamit's garden to breathe out its spices. It shows that Shulamit's sexual organs were fully ready for intercourse. She now invites Solomon to enjoy her sexually. Solomon had waited until she was ready for him, and now she signals that she is. So Solomon is invited to enjoy his garden, for she indeed belongs to him. Shulamit's private areas have been described by Solomon as a garden. Shulamit recognized it to be *his* garden.*

Answering to Shulamit's invitation, Solomon responds in 5:1a:

> I came to my garden, my sister-bride,
> I gathered my myrrh with my spices,
> I ate my honeycomb with my honey,
> I drank my wine with my milk.

In answer to Shulamit's request in the previous verse, Solomon comes into his garden, and this marks the consummation of the wedding night. The spice referred to is balsam brought to Solomon in abun-

---

* As in 2:3, some commentators see a reference to oral sex in 4:16, but this time being practiced by the groom.

dance by the Queen of Sheba (I Kings 10:16). The myrrh, balsam, honey-comb, honey, wine, and milk all point to the pinnacle of full enjoyment and satisfaction of sexual love. The gathering, eating, and drinking are all interchangeable figures describing the excitement of sexual love. While these words describe the consummation of the marriage, they would also be the words of Solomon's morning salutation to her who has now fully become his own. He verbalizes and communicates to her his pleasure. He has also fulfilled his obligation to satisfy the sexual needs of his wife (Deuteronomy 25:5).

This reflection ends with a refrain from the Daughters of Jerusalem in 5:1b:

Eat friends,
Drink and be ye drunk, O lovers.

The chorus pronounces a sanction on the wedding union and encourages them, now that they are husband and wife, to be drunk with sexual pleasure.

Summary — In reflection seven (4:1–5:1) we come again to the wedding night itself. Solomon begins by praising her beauty going from the general to the specific. He praises her eyes, hair (4:1), teeth (4:2), lips, mouth, temples (4:3), neck (4:4), and breasts (4:5). He has thus described the seven-fold beauty of his bride. Having surveyed the beauty of his new wife, he is anxious to have their first intercourse as he gazes on her pubic area (4:6). Having extolled the specific features of his bride, he concludes that all of her shares the beauty. He is totally satisfied with his bride (4:7). In his ecstatic state he invites her to go with him to Lebanon and then to descend with him from the steep heights of the mountains for even more ecstatic experiences (4:8).

Up to now he has praised her for the outward beauties which he saw, but now he begins to extol the beauties of her love by what he experiences in their first intercourse (4:9-11). He compares Shulamit to a locked garden and spring to which no one but the rightful owner can enter, and to a sealed fountain shut up against all impurities. Thus Shulamit up to now has been a virgin (4:12). It is her that Solomon now passionately desires and only by her will he be satisfied. He describes the lubrication process which will allow for the satisfaction of what he now desires (4:13-15).

Next Shulamit speaks declaring to him that her sexual organs are fully ready for intercourse with her natural secretions having performed their tasks. He waited until she was ready. Signaling that she is ready for him, she now invites him to enjoy her fully sexually (4:16).

Solomon answers Shulamit's invitation, and in the morning he greets her with a statement of his enjoyment declaring that she has now become wholly his own (5:1a). The reflection ends with the

Daughters of Jerusalem declaring and pronouncing sanction on their sexual union, love and experiences (5:1b).

Application — Two previous applications are re-emphasized here. First is the importance of verbalizing to your mate what you like about your mate. The frequency with which this has been emphasized shows the importance of this aspect of the marriage relationship. A second application being repeated is the importance of learning proper foreplay for the purpose of arousing the passions for the total enjoyment of the sex act.

The third application focuses on the importance of virginity. Shulamit entered the marriage as a virgin totally reserved for her mate. Solomon could look at her and know that no other man had enjoyed her the way he is about to now. The obvious teaching is that the believer should enter the marriage relationship as a virgin. But we live in a day of loose morality and the existence of virgins at the time of marriage is becoming more and more rare. Many single Christians today have already lost their virginity before accepting Christ, and this is one area that cannot be rectified. But at the same time, if one finds himself or herself in this position, it is necessary to remember that the believer is now a new creature in Christ, and all sins have been forgiven. One has been purified by Christ and is now to act as if one was still a virgin and reserved totally for the future mate. One must not allow the purification received with salvation to be marred but to live like a virgin reserved for the mate God has chosen. It is impossible to become a virgin again, but one can become *as* one from this point on and enter into all the joys of sexual union at marriage.

A fourth application comes from Shulamit's recognition that what had been *her* "garden" was now *his* with the consummation of the marriage. Her body, especially sexually, was now his as his was now her's. This is the same point Paul makes in I Corinthians 7:1-5 and the lesson is that one mate has the obligation of sexually satisfying the other mate because the ownership of the body has been transferred to the other upon marriage. Withholding sexual satisfaction from a mate is forbidden by Scripture.

With this, the first part of the Song of Solomon comes to an end. The whole first part dealt with the meeting, courtship, marriage, and wedding night of Solomon and Shulamit.

But once the marriage takes place, there are sexual adjustments that must be dealt with within the marriage. The second part of the book deals with this.

The second part will discuss two areas of adjustment. First is the area of sexual problems that arise in the marriage, and this is the issue in the fourth idyll. The second area of adjustment concerns experimentation with new types and acts of sexual activity in the marriage, and this is the concern of the fifth and final idyll.

PART TWO

SEXUAL ADJUSTMENTS IN MARRIAGE

5:2–8:14

CHAPTER FOUR

THE FOURTH IDYLL: SEXUAL PROBLEM REFLECTIONS
5:2–6:9

The fourth idyll deals with the adjustments resulting from marriage problems and conflicts in the realm of sexual relations.

Reflection Eight: Shulamit's Troubled Dream of Love Refused

5:2–6:3

In this reflection, as in the fifth reflection, Shulamit has a troubled dream. In the fifth reflection a distressing dream came many times, caused by the very real and long winter's separation during their court-ship days. This dream in reflection eight occurs only once and is caused by a problem in the marriage relationship resulting from a lack of sexual adjustment. Shulamit dreams of refusing Solomon's sexual advances and of losing and finding him again. This is only a dream and all the particulars need not have actually occurred, but a very real problem makes itself evident in the dream.

In 5:2 Shulamit describes Solomon's approach to her:

> I was sleeping,
> But my heart kept waking;
> The voice of my lover, knocking:
> Open for me my sister, my love,
> My dove, my perfect one;
> For my head is filled with dew,
> My locks with drips of the night.

To sleep while the heart is awake signifies a dream. Shulamit dreams that her beloved seeks admittance to her. He comes a long way, and he comes at night. The dew in his hair makes it evident that it is springtime or summer. He is asking with no expectation of delay. The word for lover is *dod,* pointing to sexual love. As Solomon approaches her, he refers to her as "my sister," that is, one of equal rank, and "my love." The Hebrew word here is *ra'eyah.* It singles her out as one freely chosen by him for intimate relationship. By "my dove" Solomon sees Shulamit as the one loved by him on account of her purity, simplicity, and loveliness, traits he mentioned earlier in the Song of Solomon. Finally she is "my perfect one." She is the one upon whom Solomon's love and devotion is centered without any division of loyalty.

In these words Solomon approaches Shulamit asking her to open herself to him. This is Solomon's sexual advance to her.

However, Shulamit refuses Solomon's advances on the basis of the excuse found in 5:3:

> I have put off my undergarment,
>> How shall I dress it (again)?
> I have washed my feet,
>> How shall I soil them (again)?

Shulamit is already lying in bed. Her undergarment is off showing that she is sleeping in the nude in bed, which was quite customary in the ancient world. Furthermore, her feet are washed. In the Middle East people wore sandals, and in the course of the day the feet became soiled with dust and dirt. So prior to bedtime, the feet would be washed.

Shulamit's response is that she is laying in bed, her feet are already washed, her undergarment is off, and she is quite unwilling to get up. To do so would mean that she would soil again that which had been washed and have to put on again that which had been taken off. Even for Solomon's sake, she is unwilling to do that which is disagreeable to her.

It should be remembered that what is happening is only a dream, but one based on reality. Faulty excuses have actually been given in rejection of sexual advances.

The next verse, 5:4, describes Solomon's attempt to get to her:

> My lover sent forth his hand through the hole,
>> And my feelings were moved for him.

Solomon, so very anxious to be with his wife, stretches his hand through the hole in the door, either in order to try to open it or as a plea to her to open the door. Regardless, Solomon's efforts to have the door opened by putting his hand through the lattice demonstrate his longing for Shulamit.

Meanwhile Shulamit, seeing the longing, begins to respond. The Hebrew word translated "my feelings" literally means "my bowels," which is the biblical concept of the seat of the tenderest emotions and marked expression of deep sympathy (cf. Isaiah 63:15, Psalm 40:11).

So Shulamit has begun to respond, but it is too late. By now Solomon has given up and departed, as 5:5-6a shows:

> (5)   I arose to open for my lover;
>>   And my hand dripped with myrrh,
>>   And my fingers with liquid myrrh.
> (6a) I opened for my lover,
>>   But my lover was turned away, gone.

Shulamit arose to open the door. As her hands touched the bolt of the door, they became wet with liquid myrrh. Liquid myrrh is myrrh that flows over, that drops of itself. In a tree it refers to that which begins to flow when an incision is made in the bark. This act may refer to a custom of a lover placing perfumed ointment or oil on the bolt of a girl's door when he comes and she is not in. Solomon came perfumed with costly myrrh as for a festival, for to be with Shulamit again was to Solomon a feast indeed! Some of the myrrh dropped off on the handle of the bolt of the door at the time Solomon stretched his hand through the lattice window. For all practical purposes, she may as well not have been home.

By the time she opened the door, Solomon had already departed. The Hebrew word is a strong one meaning *to turn aside, to take a different direction, to turn oneself away.* It points to the fact that Solomon completely turned away from Shulamit in utter disappointment over her failure to open up to him as well as her giving such flimsy excuses.

She now runs out into the streets of Jerusalem to search for him in 5:6b-7:

> (6b) My soul went out as he spoke:
>> I sought him but did not find him,
>> I called him but he did not answer me.
> (7) The watchmen found me,
>> They who go around the city,
>> They smote me,
>> They wounded me,
>> They lifted up my upper garment from upon me,
> The watchmen of the walls.

The expression "my soul went out" means *to be deeply impressed.* She now recognized that she did not respond properly to the deep impression of his loving words. So she quickly dressed and ran out to find him. As she seeks him, she fails to find him. As she calls for him, she hears no answer.

In the course of wandering around the city, the night watchmen find her and, mistaking her for a prostitute, treat her roughly. In order to escape arrest, she leaves her upper garment and manages to get away from them. This was similar to Joseph's experience in Genesis 39:12, except that in the case of Shulamit it was only her outer robe that was left behind.

Shulamit next turns to the Daughters of Jerusalem and implores their aid in 5:8:

> I adjure you, Daughters of Jerusalem,
>> If you find my lover,
>> What shall you tell him?
>> That I am love sick.

She attempts to recruit the aid of the Daughters of Jerusalem to help her find Solomon. If they do find him, they are to tell him that she is love sick for him and will respond to his advances. Her attitude has changed.

In 5:9 the Daughters of Jerusalem respond:

> What is your lover from (another) lover,
> > The beautiful one among women?
> What is your lover from (another) lover,
> > That you adjure us thus?

The Daughters of Jerusalem respond by asking what makes Shulamit's husband so special that they should bother to help her in her search. What is so special about Solomon that Shulamit so pleadingly implores them to aid her in finding him?

Shulamit responds in 5:10-16:

> (10) My lover is dazzling white and red (ruddy),
> > > Distinguished by a banner among ten thousand.
> (11) His head is precious fine gold,
> > His locks are hill upon hill
> > > Black as the raven.
> (12) His eyes are like doves,
> > > Beside streams of water;
> > > > Washed with milk,
> > > > Sitting in fulness.
> (13) His cheeks are a bed of balsam,
> > > Towers of spicy plants.
> > His lips are lilies,
> > > Dripping liquid myrrh.
> (14) His hands are cylinders of gold,
> > > Filled with topaz.
> > His abdomen is carved ivory,
> > > Covered with sapphires.
> (15) His legs are pillars of marble,
> > > Set upon bases of fine gold.
> > His aspect is like Lebanon,
> > > Chosen like cedars.
> (16) His palate is most sweetnesses,
> > > And all of him is lovelinesses;
> > This is my lover and this is my friend,
> > > O Daughters of Jerusalem.

In answer to the inquiry or sarcastic questions of the Daughters of Jerusalem, Shulamit answers and points out in detail why Solomon is so special to her as over against all others.

She begins with a general description in verse 10. His appearance combines the dazzling whiteness of his flesh with the redness of his blood against that flesh. Thus Solomon was white and ruddy, a mark of royalty in Lamentations 4:7. He is "bannered out" or marked out by this from among ten thousand.

Next Shulamit begins to describe specific features of Solomon. In verse 11 Solomon's head is like gold that is both precious and fine. The Hebrew word means fine gold guarded as a jewel (Proverbs 25:12), and a gold that is pure and free from all inferior metals (I Kings 10:18). Solomon's hair is like rolling hill country from his neck upwards; it forms waves in lines as hill upon hill. In strong contrast to his whiteness and redness, his hair is very black.

In verse 12 Solomon's eyes are moist and washed in milk, that is, his pupils are swimming in the clear whites of his eyes. In verse 13 his cheeks are a flower bed planted with sweet scented flowers and that which comes from his lips is precious liquid myrrh.

In verse 14 his hands are like cylinders of gold while his finger-nails are like imbedded topaz. His abdomen is like a work of art formed of ivory with sapphires placed in it. In verse 15 his legs are like pillars of marble while his feet are as gold. His entire aspect is as majestic as the Lebanon towering over Galilee and precious like the choice cedars.

In verse 16 his palate, that is, his organ of speech (cf. Job 6:30, Proverbs 5:3, 8:7) issues only in sweetnesses (plural of majesty or amplification). Shulamit concludes her description of Solomon by pointing out that all of him is lovelinesses (plural of majesty or amplification). "This is my lover" Shulamit concludes, "this is my friend."

Thus, regardless of the marriage problems between them, in public Shulamit refrains from criticizing Solomon but builds him up instead. She is still catching those little foxes!

Once again the Daughters of Jerusalem respond in 6:1, but this time with a different tone:

> Where is your lover gone,
>   The beautiful one among women?
> Where has your lover turned,
>   And we shall seek him with you?

Shulamit's description of Solomon has aroused their interest, and they are now eager to help her in her search for him. Indeed this is no ordinary husband! They now see why Solomon is so special to her above all the others.

But as the dream comes to an end, the help of the Daughters of Jerusalem is no longer needed for Solomon suddenly reappears in 6:2-3 as Shulamit speaks:

> (2) My lover is gone down to his garden,
>   To the beds of balsam;
>   To feed in the gardens,
>   And to pluck lilies.
> (3) I am my lover's,
>   And my lover is mine,
>   The shepherd among the lilies.

In the dream, Solomon suddenly reappears. "My lover is gone down to his garden" means that Solomon has come back to her, for the garden is Shulamit herself (4:12-15, 5:1). This indicates that Solomon has suddenly shown up and they are reunited.

The dream ends with the reunion refrain of verse three declaring that they belong to each other.

Summary — In reflection eight (5:2–6:3) Solomon and Shulamit begin to adjust sexually in marriage. At one point she refused Solomon's late night sexual advances, and this brings on a dream of Shulamit losing her beloved. It begins with a description of Solomon seeking admission to her late at night (5:2), but she refuses his sexual advances with flimsy excuses (5:3). As Solomon continues to try and show his longing for her, Shulamit is finally moved for him (5:4). When she opens the door, she finds him gone and runs out to try to find him. She calls his name but hears no answer (5:6). The watchmen of the walls find her and treat her badly, beating her because they mistake her for a prostitute (5:7).

Shulamit escapes and requests help from the Daughters of Jerusalem (5:8) who respond by asking what was so special about her lover that she thus wishes to press them into service (5:9). So she begins her description of Solomon (5:10) covering his head, hair (5:11), eyes (5:12), cheeks, lips (5:13), hands, abdomen (5:14), legs, feet (5:15) and palate (5:16a), and concluding that he is indeed majestically superior to all other lovers (5:16b). The Daughters of Jerusalem now respond that they do indeed see why he is so special to her and offer to help her find him (6:1). But at this point in the dream, Solomon suddenly reappears and they are reunited (6:2). The dream and the reflection end with a description of the reunion (6:3).

Application — Four applications can be derived from this reflection.

The first involves the necessity of sexual adjustments upon entering marriage. While proper attitudes can and should be developed before entering the marriage relationship, there is no allowance for practice in advance. The introduction to sexual relations is also an introduction to a learning experience. Mistakes will be made and should be recognized for what they are. Eventually, however, in the course of time, both husband and wife, teaching each other and learning from each other, should be able to attain a satisfying sexual adjustment. But it will take work and both partners will have to work at it.

A second application arises from Shulamit's failure to properly respond to Solomon's advances in the way she should have — a common occurrence in marriage. The basic principle to follow is never to refuse a husband's sexual advances unless circumstances demand it or call for it. A wife must learn to respond to her husband's real need. However, when circumstances do call for a refusal or delay, the wife must not use lame excuses as Shulamit did. Shulamit's attitude in this reflection is shared by many wives today. Tim Timmons in his book *Maximum Marriage* (pg. 114) quotes a letter one husband wrote after a frustrating year of having his advances refused:

To My Loving Wife,

During the past year I have tried to make love to you 365 times. I have succeeded only thirty-six times; this is an average of once every ten days. The following is a list of the reasons why I did not succeed more often: It was too late, too early, too hot, or too cold. It would waken the children, the company in the next room, or the neighbors whose windows were open. You were too full; or you had a headache, backache, toothache or the giggles. You pretended to be asleep or were not in the mood. You had on your mudpack. You watched the late TV show; I watched the late TV show; or the baby was crying.

During the times I did succeed the activity was not entirely satisfactory for a variety of reasons. Six times you chewed gum the whole time; on occasion you watched TV the whole time. Often you told me to hurry up and get it over with. A few times I tried to waken you to tell you we were through; and one time I was afraid I had hurt you for I felt you move.

Honey, It's no wonder I drink too much.

Your Loving Husband,

When a wife is unable to respond to a husband's advances for a valid reason, she must find a way to be truthful and relay it to her husband in a way that he can understand. There are two principles a wife can follow in such cases: first, verbalize why she is unable to have sex at this time in such a way that the husband will not feel resentful or rejected, perhaps suggesting an alternate time; secondly, be willing to offer to satisfy the husband sexually some other way.

A third application applies to the husband. While Shulamit on one hand put Solomon off with flimsy excuses, Solomon was not entirely fair to Shulamit either. He came home very late at night and wanted to have sexual relations immediately. Often husbands do not bother to stop and consider or be concerned over the fact that the wife may have had a very difficult day. The children may have gone out of their way to act up and frustrate their mother or housework may have caused exhaustion, leaving a woman unreceptive. While the male can be ready for sex at almost any time, the female needs to be in a proper frame of mind in order to enjoy sex. The husband must take this into account if he wishes to have satisfying sexual relations and he must prepare the way towards it by keeping his wife in a proper frame of mind so she can both respond and enjoy the relationship.

A fourth application applies to both parties and comes out of the statement Shulamit made to the Daughters of Jerusalem. The principle is one of never criticizing your mate in public. Criticisms will be necessary in a marriage, but they should only be made to each other in privacy and not in public. No matter how bad things may be at home, in public one must always build the mate up, praise one's mate or at the very least not subject the mate to criticism. Criticism in public is an extremely destructive element in a marriage. On occasion, this author has cringed in prayer meetings when women rose to give a prayer request and in doing so shred their husbands with criticism, all with the stated purpose of having people "pray more intelligently." It is no wonder that those marriages had problems! Shulamit was careful not to fall into that trap. There were problems at home, and some may have appeared to be hopeless. Every marriage will have them. There is a time to seek wise counsel for some problems. But these marital problems must never be dragged out in public so as to gain unnecessary attention. The key principle is that in public the mate must always be praised and not criticized.

Reflection Nine: The Return of Solomon

6:4-9

The dream has ended and we are now back to reality. Solomon is seen as praising his wife and shows his unconditional acceptance of Shulamit in spite of the sexual adjustment problems. Solomon is the speaker for the entire section of 6:4-9:

(4)   You are beautiful my love as Tirzah,
            Comely as Jerusalem,
            Awesome as a bannered host.
(5)   Turn away your eyes from before me,
            For they have overcome me.
        Your hair is as the flock of goats,
            Reposed downwards from Mount Gilead.
(6)   Your teeth are like a flock of shorn sheep,
            Which come up from the washing:
            That all of them have twins,
            And a lost one there is not among them.
(7)   As a piece of pomegranate are your temples
            Behind your veil.
(8)   There are sixty queens,
        And eighty concubines,
        And virgins without number.
(9)   One is she,
            My dove, my perfect one;
        One is she of her mother,
            She is the choice one of the one who bore her;
        The daughters saw her,
            And they called her blessed;
        Queens and concubines,
            And they praised her.

Solomon begins in verse four to compare Shulamit with two of the most beautiful places in Israel. Tirzah was a beautiful oasis, later to become the first capital of the Northern Kingdom (I Kings 14:17, 15:21,33, 16:8,23). Shulamit is as beautiful as the oasis of Tirzah, and as becoming and pleasing as Jerusalem. Shulamit's beauty and comeliness together are as awesome as an army about to enter into battle fully confident of victory. Solomon is totally vanquished by her beauty and comeliness.

In verse 5a he cries out against the overcoming nature of her look. The Hebrew word here is found in the *hiphil* stem and means *to press overpoweringly against one, to infuse terror*. Such are the effects of Shulamit's beauty on her husband.

The words in 5b-7 are the same as those found on the wedding night (4:1b-2,3b). Solomon now repeats these words to her in spite of her poor performance the night when she refused him. Solomon still treats her the same, showing his love for her is not based on her performance. He loves her now as much as he loved her on the wedding night. To him she is still as beautiful as a bride, and his love is still unchanged. She is not treated as being on a performance basis.

In verses 8-9 Solomon compares Shulamit to the other women in the palace. Queens were the legal wives who were to produce children, and there were sixty of these. Concubines were those skilled in sexual performance, and there were eighty of these. These numbers show that the Song of Solomon was written in an early part of Solomon's reign, for in the end he had 700 wives and 300 concubines (I Kings 11:3). The virgins were those who were prospective concubines.

This loved wife had more to offer than the sexual experts, be they concubines or prostitutes. Shulamit towered over all of them. Shulamit was the unique one of her mother so that even other relatives praised her. She was also praised by the other queens and concubines, even though she was their competitor. Shulamit was preferred over the legal wives and over the sexually expert concubines.

Summary — In reflection nine (6:4-9) we are again back to reality, and in spite of the tension in the previous reflection, they are reunited. Solomon describes her beauty again and uses many of the same words he had used on the wedding night, showing that he loves her now just as much as he loved her then (6:4-7). Although Solomon at this time had sixty other wives, eighty concubines, and an innumerable number of virgins to choose from, he still preferred Shulamit above all others, for she was unique from among all the others (6:8-9).

Application — This reflection lends itself to two important applications in addition to the oft repeated importance of verbalizing to one's mate what one appreciates and likes.

The first application is to never put your mate on a performance basis and make love conditional to it. The words of Solomon to Shulamit after the problems of the previous reflection were the same words he used on the wedding night, showing that he did not put Shulamit on a performance basis but loved her unconditionally in spite of her poor performance the night before. In the same way, our love commitment to our mate must be unconditional and never based on performance. If one loves the mate unconditionally and not on the basis of performance, it will keep one from criticizing the mate in public. The mate must be made to understand the unconditional nature of one's love. If it is based on performance, tension is bound to enter the marriage relationship. Again, the unconditional nature of this love must be verbalized.

The second application is the importance of totally satisfying the mate sexually so that there is never any desire to look elsewhere. A wife should cultivate her uniqueness so as to be attractive in many ways. The married woman should have more to offer than professional prostitutes or mistresses. The same holds true for the husband. Hence the importance of learning what will totally satisfy one's mate and how to meet that need. This also re-emphasizes the importance of previous applications concerning the need to pay attention to physical appearances such as weight, clothes, perfumes, etc. There is an abundance of information available in the books listed in the appendix.

CHAPTER FIVE

THE FIFTH IDYLL: THE RETURN TO GALILEE REFLECTIONS
6:10–8:14

Whereas the previous idyll dealt with sexual adjustments arising out of a specific marriage problem, the fifth idyll deals with sexual adjustments related to the trying of new techniques in the enjoyment of sex. This comprises the final four reflections, all of which occur in the springtime.

Reflection Ten: The Dance of the Mahanaim
6:10–7:10

In this reflection Shulamit has gone down to the royal nut gardens to reflect on the vegetation now beginning to blossom. As she is returning to the palace, she encounters the Daughters of Jerusalem, and they ask in 6:10:

> Who is this, the one looking like the dawn,
>   Beautiful as the full-white moon,
>   Pure as the warm sun,
>   Awesome as a bannered host?

The question starts out with "who is this," just as in 3:6. Previously the inquiry was of her who was being brought to the king, but now in 6:10 it is of her who moves in that which has become her own. Shulamit's appearance is likened to the morning dawn. She is further compared to the moon and the sun. Of the two Hebrew words for moon, the word chosen in this text is the one which emphasizes the whiteness of the moon rather than the other which emphasizes the moon as yellow. Of the two Hebrew words for sun, the one chosen in this text emphasizes the warmness of the sun, whereas the other pictures the sun as unwearied.

As with Solomon, the Daughters of Jerusalem liken Shulamit's beauty to a bannered army about to go into battle confident of victory. Shulamit appears as the morning dawn that breaks through the darkness of the night, beautiful like the silvery white moon, pure as the warm sun. Everything emphasizes the freshness of the woman.

To this Shulamit responds in 6:11-12:

> (11) Unto the nut garden I went down,
>   To see the shrubs of the valley brook,
>   To see the budding of the vine,
>   And the pomegranates flowering.
> (12) I did not know my soul lifted me up,
>   Set me (among) the chariots of my princely people.

Shulamit responds that on this spring morning she had gone down to look at what reminded her most of home. She went down for the purpose of observing the state of the vegetation in the garden of walnuts.

The point in verse 12 is that because she had been so quickly and suddenly elevated from a country peasant girl to being the wife of the king, she has still not fully acculturated to the city life or to the royal life of the palace. Hence, she went to the place that reminded her most of home — the royal gardens.

As she turns to continue on her way back to the palace, the Daughters of Jerusalem speak up once again in 6:13a:

Return, Return, O Shulamit,
Return, Return, and we will gaze on you.

Shulamit has continued her walk back to the palace when the Daughters of Jerusalem call for her that they might find delight in looking upon her. The Hebrew word translated "gaze" means *to sink oneself into a thing looking at it, to delight (feast) one's eyes in looking at a thing.* Thus it means *to look deeply in pleasure and for pleasure.*

For the first time in the book Shulamit is addressed by name. The name is not so much a proper name as it is a name of descent pointing to Shulamit's place of origin. From the name it is clear that Shulamit is from the town of Shunem, known later as Shulem (the *l* and *n* sounds often interchanged in Hebrew and other Semitic languages) and today as Sulam. It was a town of the tribe of Issachar (Joshua 19:17-18) located at the foot of the Hill of Moreh, also known as the Little Hermon. Shunem was noted for its beautiful women, for not only did Shulamit come from there, but also the beautiful Abishag of I Kings 1:3-4. The Shunamite woman, Elisha's hostess, also lived there (II Kings 4:8-11).

Thus Shulamit was from Shunem or Shulem and she was a member of the tribe of Issachar. Her home was in Galilee and not in Lebanon as some commentators would have it. The name "Shulamit" does two things in this book: it gives her place of origin, and it gives the feminine form of the name "Solomon."

Shulamit responds to the call of the Daughters of Jerusalem in 6:13b:

Why would you gaze on the Shulamite?

Humble as she is, Shulamit still fails to fully comprehend her own beauty and the effect it has on others, especially on her husband. So to this the Daughters of Jerusalem reply in 6:13c:

As the Dance of the Mahanaim.

Some have interpreted the Dance of the Mahanaim to be a reference back to Genesis 32:1-2 saying it refers to angelic dancing. But there is no example anywhere in the Scriptures of angels dancing. More likely it refers to an erotic dance, for this is exactly what follows in the context. The Daughters of Jerusalem call Shulamit back for they wish her to perform an erotic dance. It must be remembered that the chorus is imaginary in the lyric idyll, and they are not really actors in the play. The imaginary chorus is brought in to explain a situation, to give a warning, or to allow for a dialogue to take place or, as is the case here, to set the stage for what follows.

The request by the Daughters of Jerusalem for an erotic dance by Shulamit is really Solomon's request, for as the following verses make clear, Shulamit is indeed dancing erotically.

In 7:1-5 Shulamit is viewed as dancing, but the chorus has disappeared from the scene. She is dancing before Solomon alone. She is either dancing in the nude or wearing see-through veils. At any rate, Solomon is able to see all of her, and he begins to describe what he sees as Shulamit is dancing the Dance of the Mahanaim and displaying all her charms:

(1) How beautiful are your feet in sandals,
         O prince's daughter;
     The curves (vibrations) of your thighs are like jewels,
         The work of the hands of an artist.
(2) Your navel is a rounded basin,
         Without the lack of mingled wine.
     Your belly is a heap of wheat,
         Set about with lilies.
(3) Your two breasts
         Are like two fawns,
         Twins of a gazelle.
(4) Your neck is like the tower of ivory.
     Your eyes like the pools in Heshbon,
         By the gates of Bat Rabbim.
     Your neck is like the tower of Lebanon,
         Looking towards Damascus.
(5) Your head upon you is like Carmel,
     And the flowing locks of your head like purple;
         A king is captive in the tresses.

As Shulamit dances before him, Solomon begins to detail the beauties of his wife. The Hebrew word translated "feet" signifies *step and foot,* portraying her as dancing with her feet going back and forth. In describing the vibrations of her dancing thighs, Solomon points to the manifold twistings and windings of the upper part of her body by means of the thigh joints, for the Hebrew words signify movements of a circular kind.

The Hebrew word translated "curves" refers to the thighs in motion and not the beauty curves of the thighs at rest. The entire Hebrew passage keeps pointing towards a dancing female. The thighs in motion are described as jewels. The Hebrew word signifies female ornaments consisting of gold, silver, and precious stones. This figure is used by Solomon because the bending of the thighs and loins full of life and beauty are like the free swinging of such ornaments when connected to a chain. Thus the legs of Shulamit are very much in dancing motion.

In verse two the navel is described as being in the shape of a half moon with the roundness of a basin, the kind of basin used for the mixing of fine wines. The belly or waist is described as a "heap of wheat" which points to the color of her flesh, a mixture of wheat yellow along with some lily white.

In verse three he describes her two breasts in the same way as in 4:5, and the reader can look there for commentary.

In verse four her neck is likened to a tower of ivory, her eyes are like moist pools, and her nose is well defined.

Verse five completes the description with Shulamit's head and hair in motion. Her head is majestic, and her hair appears red-purple. Solomon is totally captivated by her and sees himself as a prisoner in the tresses of her hair.

With this the dancing ends and lovemaking begins in 7:6-9a:

(6)   How you are beautiful,
        And how you are pleasant,
            O love, in the delights.
(7)   This your stature is likened to a palm tree,
            And your breasts to clusters.
(8)   I said:
            I will go up into the palm tree,
            I will take hold in its branches,
        And let your breasts be as clusters of the vine,
            And the smell of your nose like apples.
(9a)   And your palate as the good wine.

In verse six, following the erotic dance of Shulamit before her husband as a new technique of sexual enjoyment, lovemaking begins.

In verse seven, Shulamit is standing before Solomon, and he surveys her from head to foot comparing her to a palm tree. The Hebrew word translated "palm tree" refers to the female flower out of which develops large clusters of juicy sweet fruit. Shulamit's breasts are compared to such clusters. The Hebrew word translated "clusters" refers to the dark brown or golden yellow cluster which grows at the summit of the branches and beautifies the appearance of the palm tree. So as Shulamit stands tall and straight before Solomon after completing her erotic dance, Solomon compares her to a palm tree and notes that her body is further beautified by her breasts.

In verse eight Solomon is viewed as climbing the palm tree as he and Shulamit unite in sexual enjoyment. The thought is that of securing possession of her and of the enjoyment the erotic dance had promised. The picture is that of fertilizing the palm tree, hence making love to her.

The words of Solomon close with the statement of verse 9a which essentially says the same thing as the words of the famous song "kisses sweeter than wine."

At this point Shulamit interrupts Solomon's words with her own in 7:9b:

Going down for my lover smoothly,
Moving the lips of the sleeping.

Shulamit interrupts Solomon's statement about the wine to complete the figure begun by him. Bad tasting wine sticks to the palate. Good tasting wine goes down smoothly. The wine is a figure of sexual love, and like good wine that has been sipped in the course of an evening, the pleasing satisfaction still hovers long after they have gone to sleep.

As this reflection comes to an end with the lovemaking completed, Shulamit states in 7:10:

I am my lover's
    And upon me is his desire.

At the conclusion of lovemaking Shulamit declares herself to belong to Solomon alone, just as Solomon's desire is only for her.

This reflection has been concerned with sexual adjustments in the realm of experimentation with a new technique, the use of an erotic dance. The following reflections will center on another technique.

Summary — In reflection ten (6:10–7:10) we have a description of the Dance of the Mahanaim. It is springtime again, and Shulamit has gone down to the royal gardens. As she leaves them, she is greeted by the Daughters of Jerusalem (6:10). She responds to their question by stating that she went down to the royal gardens to see the state of the vegetation (6:11). She has all of her life been a country girl who now has suddenly been lifted up to the position of being the king's wife, and she has not as yet fully acclimated to city life and life in the royal palace. Hence, she went down to the place that reminded her of home (6:12). As she continues her trek to the palace, the Daughters of Jerusalem call after her to be able to gaze at her beauty some more (6:13a). Humble as she is and failing to see her own real beauty, she responds by asking them what they could possibly see in a simple country girl from Shunem (6:13b). The Daughters of Jerusalem reply that they could see in her all the beauties that one sees in a woman performing the Dance of the Mahanaim (6:13c).

Now the scene changes and Shulamit is indeed doing the Dance of the Mahanaim, but it is being done before Solomon. As she dances displaying her charms, Solomon describes the beauty of her dancing. He describes the movement of her feet, thighs (7:1), navel, waist (7:2), breasts (7:3), neck, eyes, nose (7:4), head and hair (7:5). Solomon is totally captivated by her. When the dance is over, they begin to make love. He compares her to a palm tree with clusters ready to be fertilized and speaks of his possession of that palm tree in sexual love (7:6-8). Solomon concludes that their love is like good tasting wine (7:9a).

Shulamit continues the figure of the good wine by describing it as going down smoothly, for love is like good wine sipped with pleasing satisfaction which delightfully hovers about the loving sleepers throughout the night (7:9b). This reflection ends with Shulamit's declaration that Solomon's desire is for her alone, and she is only his (7:10).

Application — The one key application in this reflection is that of encouraging creativity in sexual relations. One need not necessarily do the very things that Solomon and Shulamit did. The principle is that all things are permissible if they are agreeable to both parties, but all things are not mandatory. A couple should not allow themselves to get into a rut in their sexual activities any more than in any other sphere of their lives. Different techniques of sex should be tried and tested in order to bring variety and spice into the sex life. It should be remembered that no kind of sexual activity between a married couple is sinful or unclean as long as these two standards are met: it is agreeable to both parties and it meets the mate's needs. At times it will be impossible to know the above until it is tried at least once. But a part of sexual adjustment in marriage involves just that. In all, creativity should be applied and variety brought in to make the whole marriage relationship more exciting.

Reflection Eleven: Shulamit's Desire to Visit Home
7:10–8:4

Because of the longing for home in the previous reflection, Shulamit asks Solomon to come with her to visit her home for two purposes: first, to renew the love covenant in the very place where their courtship began; and secondly, to make love there, which they could not do before since they were still unmarried.

The request for the trip for the purpose of trying a new technique comes in 7:11-13:

(11)   Come my lover,
      Let us go out to the country,
      Let us lodge in the villages.
(12)   Let us rise early to the vineyards,
      Let us see if the vines have budded,
        The vine blossoms have opened,
        The pomegranates are in flower.
      There will I give my loves to you.
(13)   The mandrakes are giving fragrance,
      And over our doors are all kinds of excellent fruit:
        New and old
        I kept for you, my lover.

In verse 11 Shulamit makes her request to visit home. The villages refer to the towns in which they will sleep on the way to Galilee. In verse 12 she makes clear she wants to visit the very country where they courted. There she promises to give "my loves" to him. The Hebrew word is *dod*, and it is in the plural number referring to sexual loves. She is seeking to be able to make sexual love in the outdoors several times—something possible in the country but not in a city like Jerusalem. This is something they were unable to do during courtship and still could not do in the city, but they would be free to do it now in the country.

In order to encourage Solomon to attempt this, Shulamit points out in verse 13 that the mandrakes are in flower and are giving fragrance. The Hebrew word for mandrakes is *dodaim* which has the same root as that of sexual love. Mandrakes are known as the "lover's flower" and also as "love apples." It is a whitish green flower with yellow apples the size of nutmeg and has a strong and pleasant odor. The fruits and roots were used as an aphrodisiac and were thought to stimulate sexual arousal. This is the background to the events of Genesis 30:14-16:

> And Reuben went in the days of wheat harvest, and found mandrakes in the field, and brought them unto his mother Leah. Then Rachel said to Leah, Give me, I pray thee, of thy son's mandrakes. And she said unto her, Is it a small matter that thou hast taken away my husband? and wouldest thou take away my son's mandrakes also? And Rachel said, Therefore he shall lie with thee tonight for thy son's mandrakes. And Jacob came from the field in the evening, and Leah went out to meet him, and said, Thou must come in unto me; for I have surely bought thee with my son's mandrakes. And he lay with her that night.

And so with the mandrakes blossoming in the fields of Galilee to stimulate sexual arousal, she urges him to go north and to try another new sexual technique by making love in the outdoors. This is the second kind of new sexual practice that Shulamit is trying out.

Shulamit continues to express her desire in 8:1-3:

(1)   Who would give you as a brother to me,
                Sucking the breast of my mother;
        I would find you outside,
        I would kiss you,
        Also, no one would despise me;
(2)   I would lead you,
        I would bring you into the house of my mother;
        You could teach me,
        I would cause you to drink spiced wine
                From the juice of my pomegranates.
(3)   His left hand is under my head,
                And his right hand embraces me.

Shulamit's wish in verse one is that he would be to her what a brother was to a sister. She does not wish that Solomon was a brother, but only *as* a brother. This is so that she could openly display her affection on him without restraint for the sake of appearance or to be treated scornfully for it. Again the emphasis is on making love outside.

As she continues to speak in verse two, Shulamit describes how she would bring him to her home that forever he might become her teacher. Shulamit wishes that she might participate in Solomon's wisdom. She recognizes how much she still comes short of being to him all that she could be. Thus there is a beautiful marriage balance in the passage. Solomon has already made it clear in the previous reflection that he is totally satisfied with Shulamit as she is. But she does not let this satisfaction keep her from trying to become a better wife.

In verse three the instruction is seen as already beginning. Carrying out the figure of a brother, she can now openly show affection in private, but only later while outside.

This reflection ends in 8:4 with the familiar refrain slightly altered to read:

> I adjure you,
>   O daughters of Jerusalem,
> Why should you arouse,
>   And why should you stir up love
> Until it will be pleased?

For the third time in the book Shulamit admonishes that sexual passion should not be aroused until it can also be satisfied. In 2:7 it was in the context of marriage: sexual passion should not be aroused unless it can be satisfied, otherwise it will lead to frustration. In 3:5 it was stated in the context of courtship: sexual passion should not be aroused for it may lead to fornication. Here in 8:4 it is in the context of a proper place: sexual passion should not be aroused in a place where it cannot be satisfied.

This reflection records Shulamit's request for Solomon to join her in a trip to her home for the purpose of trying something new.

Summary — Reflection eleven (7:11–8:4) picks up the longing Shulamit had for her country home in the previous reflection. She begins by requesting from Solomon that they get away alone together to visit her country home (7:11). There in the vineyards of Galilee they could see the vegetation beginning to spring to life and find the opportunity to make sexual love in the outdoors; something they could not do in the city (7:12). There in the fields of Galilee is an abundance of mandrakes, an aphrodisiac to nurture their sexual experience all the more (7:13).

Reflecting on the desire to be able to show her love for him in the open, Shulamit wishes Solomon could be to her like a brother upon whom she could show affection outdoors without worrying about what others may think (8:1). Then she could bring him to her home forever so that he could be her teacher. Although Solomon accepted her as she is, she recognizes that she is still not fully the wife she could be to him. A trip to the north away from the hustle and bustle of palace life will give her an opportunity to try all the more (8:2). Having made her request and Solomon consenting, they again make love (8:3). This reflection ends when, for the third time, Shulamit adjures the Daughters of Jerusalem that sexual passion should not be aroused unless it can also be satisfied (8:4). This is in the context emphasizing the place of sex. So she points out that sexual passion should not be aroused in a place where it cannot be satisfied.

Application — A number of applications are readily apparent in this reflection. First is a re-emphasis of a previous one—that of creativity in the sex life. In the previous reflection Shulamit used the technique of an erotic dance, while in this one she introduces the thought of having sex in the outdoors. Again, the point is not that we need to do everything exactly the way Solomon and Shulamit did. That is not the emphasis, and most people do not live in situations where it is possible to make love in the outdoors. But the point is that of creative experimentation and ecstasy in the sex life, and this is the whole point of the application.

The second application comes from Shulamit's attitude toward the relationship. It should be noted how often in this book it is Shulamit who takes the initiative in their sexual relationship. She has already come to realize from previous reflections that Solomon loves her unconditionally and she is not on a performance basis. But it is this very thing that stimulates her towards improvement. One can certainly learn a lesson here. When our mate has verbalized the unconditional nature of his or her love for us, one should accept and believe it, and not develop a guilt complex of being on a performance basis. But the very fact of unconditional love should not lead to complacency but to stimulation toward improvement in all areas of our life, including the sex life. It is because of unconditional love that we should try to perform better knowing that even when we fail, it has not in any way affected the love relationship which is unconditional.

The third application arises from Shulamit's third statement concerning sexual arousal. The point here is that sexual passion should not be aroused in a place where it cannot be satisfied. This limits a believing couple in the way they can learn and experiment sexually. This rules out going to those kind of movies which are sex oriented and exist for the sole purpose of sexual arousal. These are not places for Christians to learn anything, and the end result is that sexual passion is aroused in a place where it cannot be satisfied and so will lead to frustration as well as the danger of fornication or both.

The fourth application is the necessity to get away in order to be alone together. The husband should make it a practice to have one night a week set aside to be spent with the wife alone. Because of children and the telephone, it will often be necessary to go out of the house. Even if it means spending ten dollars for a babysitter leaving only two dollars for a hamburger, let it be done. The importance lies in being alone together without the usual distractions. In addition to the weekly evening, the couple should plan times to get away for an entire weekend to be by themselves. This will not always necessitate a trip out of town. Some have simply reserved a room or the bridal suite in a nearby hotel just to be alone with their mate. The aim is to get to a place where no one can reach you by dropping by or calling. This can often be done without an expensive trip out of town.

Couples often spend their two week vacations with the folks at home, but these get-togethers with the relatives are better done on long Thanksgiving, Christmas or Easter weekends. It would be far better to use all or most of those two weeks to be completely alone and doing things with each other as a couple (or as an individual family unit when the children come) for a longer extended period of time than is possible on a weekend. There are all kinds of possibilities for "getting away" for a night, a weekend or a week or more. These get aways can be creatively planned. Getting alone is a very important aspect of the marital relationship.

Reflection Twelve: The Renewal of the Love Covenant

8:5-7

In the previous reflection, Shulamit spelled out the need to get away together and to be by themselves. Solomon agreed with her. This next reflection describes the journey as they go north and the renewal of their love covenant upon their arrival.

This reflection begins with a question by the chorus in 8:5a:

> Who is this the one coming from the wilderness,
> Leaning upon her beloved?

The question starts out in the same way as in 3:6 and 6:10 and is always in reference to Shulamit. As the long journey is about to conclude, she is seen as leaning upon Solomon to support herself from the weariness of travel. The fact that they are seen as coming from the wilderness tells us that they left Jerusalem via the Jericho Road, came up the Jordan Valley, and left the wilderness by coming through the Beth Shean Pass to Shunem. It is the very same route she took when she went to Jerusalem in the wedding procession.

Solomon begins speaking in 8:5b:

> Under the apple (tree) I awakened you;
> There your mother was in travail with you,
> There she was in travail, there she bore you.

As they finally arrive in familiar territory, they come to the apple tree where she first won his love. It witnessed the beginning of their love. It was also the place where she was born. The apple tree witnessed her birth, and it also witnessed the arousal of their love.

One purpose for this trip was to renew the love covenant, and it is done now as Shulamit speaks in 8:6-7:

(6)   Set me as a seal (signet ring) upon your heart,
            As a seal (signet ring) upon your arm;
    For strong as death is love,
            Hard as Sheol is jealousy,
    Her flames are flashes of fire,
            A most vehement flame of Jehovah.
(7)   Many waters are not able to quench the love,
            And rivers cannot overflow it;
    If a man will give all the substance of his house for love,
            He will surely be despised.

With these words the love covenant is renewed. The seal or signet ring was the emblem of authority (eg. Genesis 41:42, I Kings 21:8) worn on the right hand (eg. Jeremiah 22:24) or against the heart by a string from the neck (eg. Genesis 38:18). It was a jewel from which one did not separate himself. Shulamit thus signifies that she wants to be Solomon's most prized and precious possession. He should possess her in such a way so as to never separate himself from her.

The reason for this is based on the very nature of the love about to be described. The word here is *ahavah* which includes both the concepts of *dod* and *ra'eyah* plus much more. The very nature of the love covenant between Solomon and Shulamit now about to be renewed demands that he take her in such a way that they become inseparable.

The energy of this love is compared to the energy of death and Sheol, for love and the jealousy of love are equal to it. The Hebrew word translated "strong" means *powerful*. On one hand, it can designate a person who is being attacked but cannot be overcome (eg. Numbers 13:28). On the other hand, if the powerful one is himself doing the attacking, he cannot be withstood (eg. Judges 14:18). Here death is seen as being powerful, and nothing can withstand it (cf. Jeremiah 9:21). Against death nothing can hold its ground or escape. All must eventually yield to it. The type of love Shulamit describes is as powerful as death, for it too can seize men with irresistible force. Whomever death attacks must die, and whomever love attacks must love. As death kills in relationship to everything living, even so love kills in relationship to everything else that is not the object of one's love.

The jealousy of love is hard as Sheol. Jealousy, in its proper usage, simply asserts its right of possession or ownership. Thus the jealousy of love fully takes possession of the object of love, just as Sheol takes full possession of the dead (Psalm 49:13-15). Jealousy burns against everyone who will try to violate the right of ownership.

So since love is powerful as death, Shulamit gives herself up to this love on the condition that Solomon will love only her and will be as dead to all others, and all others will be dead to him. Since the jealousy of love is also hard as Sheol, she hides in this jealousy as security against any unfaithfulness.

This kind of love, furthermore, is the very "flame of Jehovah." In Hebrew this is a flame of the most vehement kind, a flame of bright shining and fiery flashes. Love of the right kind is not a flame kindled by man but by God. This is the only place in the book where God is mentioned. He is the source of this love, and before Him the love covenant is renewed.

Furthermore, in verse seven this kind of love cannot be extinguished by many waters nor can rivers overflow it to sweep it away. No amount of adverse circumstances can extinguish this kind of love, for the flame of Jehovah is inextinguishable. Nor can this love be bought, and any attempt to buy it would be scorned and viewed as madness.

Thus nothing can change Shulamit's love for the king — not circumstances nor money. The love covenant is renewed in the very place where it was made.

Summary — In reflection twelve (8:5-7) the loving couple travel to the home of Shulamit. The chorus in Shunem asks for the identity of the ones coming, seeing the girl leaning on her beloved because of the weariness of the journey (8:5a). As they approach the village, Solomon points out the apple tree where he once found her sleeping and awakened her. This marked the beginning of their love, and so love began near the home where Shulamit was born (8:5b).

Now Shulamit wishes to renew their love covenant. She asks Solomon to possess her as he would possess a valuable signet ring from which he would never wish to depart. She wants to be his most prized possession, so that he would never separate himself from her. The energy of love is comparable to the energy of death and Sheol. He whom death assails must die, and he whom love assails must love. Love is strong as death, and so Shulamit gives herself up to this love on the condition that Solomon will love only her and that he will be dead to all others. Jealousy is as inexorable as Sheol, and Shulamit takes shelter in the jealousy of this love against any infidelity.

This kind of love, the right kind of love, is of God. He alone is the source of this love. Before Him the love covenant is renewed (8:6). This kind of love cannot be destroyed by adverse circumstances nor can this kind of love be bought with money. So neither circumstances nor money can separate her from her love for the king (8:7). And so their love covenant is renewed where it had first been made.

Application — Only one application can be deduced from this reflection, but it is an important one: the renewal of the love covenant. It is good for a couple to periodically reflect on the state of the commitment that was made during courtship and marriage and then to renew it in some way. Some couples choose to have a second wedding and honeymoon. Others have chosen different means of renewing the love commitment. Nor is there any special time of life that it should be done. In the case of Shulamit, she chose to have it done after a sufficient period of marital adjustment. This is indeed a good time to renew the commitment, but it can be done at any time a couple feels the need to do so. Another good time to renew the love commitment is after salvation. If the marriage took place before either member was a believer, God was not included in the marriage vows. So after salvation, when the biblical principles of marriage are understood, a renewal of the love covenant before the Lord is very much in order.

Whenever possible, the renewal of the marriage commitment may be made in the place of courtship as Shulamit chose to do. But this is not always possible and the renewal can be made elsewhere.

Reflection Thirteen: At Shulamit's Country Home

8:8-14

In this final reflection Shulamit arrives home with Solomon. She begins conversing with her brothers concerning her little sister in 8:8:

> We have a little sister,
> And she has no breasts;
> What shall we do for our sister,
> In the day she will be spoken for.

It is in this verse that we learn that Shulamit has a younger sister. By describing her as not having breasts, Shulamit is stating that her sister is still very young and without sexual development, and so there is no need for concern at this present time. But the question is, what will be done to protect her chastity when she is older? Thus Shulamit shows concern for the sexual development of her sister, and even more so that her sister remain pure and chaste. "In the day she will be spoken for" refers to the day when suitors come courting her (cf. I Samuel 25:39).

The brothers answer Shulamit's question of concern in 8:9:

> If she be a wall,
> We will build upon her a battlement of silver;
> And if she be a door,
> We will block upon her boards of cedar.

In the ancient world brothers often served as the nearest guardians and counselors of the sister, and in the area of marriage often had precedence over the father and mother (cf. Genesis 24:50-60, 34:1-17). In answer to Shulamit the brothers exert their authority by explaining that if the younger sister proves to be a wall, that is, inaccessible to seduction, she will be rewarded by them. Of the several Hebrew words for "wall," the one chosen here implies a wall that stands firm and withstands every assault against it. So if the sister is such a wall withstanding all immoral assaults, they will adorn her with silver: giving her the highest honor that she will deserve for her purity.

But if she proves to be like a door, which although closed is so built that it may be opened, that is, accessible to seduction, then they will apply boards of cedar. So if she is a door and accessible to seduction, they will enclose her with cedar planks, that is, watch her in such a manner that no seducers will be able to approach her and thus not give her an opportunity for any promiscuity.

In this way the brothers comfort Shulamit in her concern by telling her that they will be very careful to guard their younger sister's chastity and purity.

After these words from her brothers, Shulamit responds in 8:10:

I am a wall,
    And my breasts like towers;
Then I was in his eyes,
    As one finding peace.

The previous statement of her brothers regarding the wall reminds Shulamit of the way she was. She could declare that she was indeed a wall and inaccessible to seduction. Her breasts, unlike her sister's, were like towers, that is, fully developed and ready for love—but only with her husband. So she kept her virginity and purity. Then she was able to enter in all purity into a marriage covenant of peace with Solomon.

Shulamit now begins to see the reason behind what appeared like harsh treatment by her brothers. They were actually concerned for her chastity and wished to keep her pure for her future mate. At times this required what appeared as harsh treatment from her brothers. Should not this faithful guardianship by her brothers be rewarded? To this matter Shulamit now turns in 8:11-12 as she speaks to Solomon:

(11)   Solomon had a vineyard in Baal Hermon,
            He gave the vineyard to the keepers,
                That each one should bring for its fruit
                One thousand pieces of silver.
(12)   My vineyard, even mine, is before me;
            The one thousand for you, O Solomon,
            And two hundred to the ones keeping its fruit.

In verse 11 Shulamit reminds Solomon how he owns vineyards in the nearby area and leases them out to keepers for one thousand pieces of silver. In return Solomon pays them their earnings of twenty percent or two hundred pieces of silver. But now in verse 12, as in 1:6, she turns away from the literal vineyard to the personal vineyard which represents herself. The statement of 1:6 taken together with 8:9-12 helps to explain the entire situation. The brothers concerned for Shulamit's chastity forced her to work in the open vineyards where seduction unseen would be impossible. Thus the brothers were indeed the real protectors of the vineyard represented by Shulamit.

This vineyard of hers has now been given over freely into Solomon's possession; she is now his. This vineyard which is Shulamit also had keepers to whom Solomon is in debt, for she became his possession as a chaste and virtuous virgin. Her brothers were the real keepers of this vineyard. They were the protectors of her innocence. Therefore, they should be rewarded.

Solomon has his one thousand: Shulamit herself. Her brothers have earned their two hundred, even as the keepers of the literal vineyards in Baal Hermon received theirs. And so Shulamit provides the sustenance for her family out of her new wealth. She makes sure that they are well taken care of. Solomon does not specifically answer this request, but the tone of the passage is that he responded favorably.

Solomon speaks next in 8:13:

> O thou that dwellest in the gardens,
>> Friends are listening for your voice,
>> Cause me to hear it!

Solomon now asks Shulamit to gratify the friends of her youth and sing a song as she used to in the past. These friends are the friends of her youth when she was a shepherdess and keeper of her family vineyards. In calling her the one dwelling in the gardens, he refers to her as the one very much at home in the present surroundings. She is a country girl, and she is nature's child.

Shulamit responds to Solomon's request in 8:14:

> Flee my lover,
>> And be thou like a gazelle,
>> Or like a young one of the harts,
> On the mountains of spices.

With this verse Shulamit begins her song as the Song of Solomon comes to an end. The Hebrew word translated "flee" refers to a sense of *hastening* (cf. Job 9:25, 14:2). Here it means to flee away from all others in order to be alone.

This verse is similar to 2:17, but there the love relationship was still in the progress of courtship and so uninterrupted fellowship was not possible. Now that they are married, the summons in 8:14 is unlimited.

Thus they go outside to do that which they had planned to do in earlier reflections (7:12-13, 8:1) and disappear into the flowery hills.

Summary — In reflection thirteen (8:8-14) the couple arrive at

Shulamit's home where she had at least two brothers and one little sister. Although her sister is still too young to have had any sexual development, Shulamit expresses her concern to her brothers about how the chastity of her little sister can be protected when the time comes (8:8). Her brothers reply that they will watch her development. If she is inaccessible to seduction, they will honor her for her purity. If she is accessible to seduction, they will watch her in such a manner that no seducer will be able to approach her (8:9).

Her brothers' response reminds Shulamit as to how they had protected her in the past so that when she married Solomon she was a pure virgin (8:10). Shulamit now turns to Solomon with a request to reward her brothers for this. Solomon had many vineyards that he leased out to keepers. When the keepers had reaped the fruit and given it to Solomon, they would be given a portion of it in return for faithful service. In a similar way Shulamit was now his special vineyard, and her brothers had been her keepers giving faithful service. Therefore, they should be rewarded as well (8:11-12). Apparently Solomon agreed.

Shulamit's friends from her childhood are in the house, having come to see her and to hear her singing. So Solomon asks her to satisfy them and to sing (8:13). Shulamit begins her song as she leads Solomon outside leaving all the others behind in the house. They disappear into the flowered hills to practice outdoors that which they came up north to do—to make love (8:14). With this the Song of Solomon comes to an end.

Application — This last reflection yields two applications. The first is a reaffirmation of the importance of entering into marriage a virgin, for the one doing so receives the greater honor.

The second application is the importance of being an example to others of proper attitudes towards sex. In this reflection, Shulamit served as an example to her younger sister. Shulamit's brothers watched her development and took proper precautions at proper times. Children often reflect the sexual attitudes of their parents. If the parents view sex within marriage positively, their children are less likely to have negative attitudes. If a mother views sex as simply a necessary evil, the daughter is apt to enter into marriage with the same attitude. If the father views sex as a means of male gratification without real regard for the pleasure and personhood of the wife, the son is apt to enter into marriage with the same concepts. The end product is a repetition of their parents' unhappiness in the marriage. Christian couples should develop a healthy and biblical attitude toward sexual union. Such an attitude will provide a good example for their children. By becoming examples of both virtue and proper attitudes towards sexual relations, the parents are laying the foundations for the success of their children's future marriage.

APPENDIX

Recommended Books and Tapes on Marriage

Dillow, Linda. *Creative Counterpart.* (Nashville, Tennessee: Thomas Nelson Inc., Publishers, 1977). [Study guide available].

Dobson, James. *Straight Talk To Men And Their Wives.* (Waco, Texas: Word Books, 1980).

Dobson, James. *What Wives Wish Their Husbands Knew About Women.* (Wheaton, Illinois: Tyndale House Publishers, Inc., 1975).

LaHaye, Tim and Beverly. *The Act of Marriage: The Beauty of Sexual Love.* (Grand Rapids, Michigan: Zondervan Publishing House, 1976).

Littauer, Florence. *After Every Wedding Comes A Marriage.* (Eugene, Oregon: Harvest House Publishers, 1981). [Study guide available].

Mayhall, Jack and Carole. *Marriage Takes More Than Love.* (Colorado Springs, Colorado: NavPress, 1978).

Meredith, Don. *Becoming One.* (Nashville, Tennessee: Thomas Nelson Publishers, 1979).

Rice, Shirley. *Physical Unity In Marriage: A Woman's View.* (Norfolk, Virginia: The Tabernacle Church of Norfolk, 1973).

Swindoll, Charles R. *Strike The Original Match.* (Portland, Oregon: Multnomah Press, 1980).

Timmons, Tim. *Biblical Lovemaking.* [Tapes]. (Santa Ana, California: One Way Library, 1976).

Timmons, Tim. *God's Plan For Your Marriage.* (Grand Rapids, Michigan: Baker Book House, 1974).

Timmons, Tim. *Maximum Marriage.* (Old Tappan, New Jersey: Fleming H. Revell Company, 1976). [available on tape].

Wheat, Ed, M.D. *Before The Wedding Night* [Tapes]. (Springdale, Arkansas: Scriptural Counseling, Inc., 1982).

Wheat, Ed, M.D. *Love Life: For Every Married Couple.* (Grand Rapids, Michigan: Zondervan Publishing House, 1980). [available on tape].

Wheat, Ed, M.D. and Gaye. *Intended For Pleasure.* (Old Tappan, New Jersey: Fleming H. Revell Company, 1977). [portions available on tape "Sex Technique and Sex Problems In Marriage"]